Historic Gleanings in Windham County, Connecticut

Ellen Douglas Larned

BIBLIOBAZAAR

HISTORIC GLEANINGS

IN

WINDHAM COUNTY, CONNECTICUT

BY

ELLEN D. LARNED

AUTHOR OF

"HISTORY OF WINDHAM COUNTY."

PROVIDENCE, R. I.

PRESTON AND ROUNDS COMPANY

1899

CONTENTS

HISTORIC GLEANINGS IN WINDHAM COUNTY.

I.

SPENT LIGHTS.[*]

There is nothing more surprising to the student of
history than the apparent capriciousness of the chance
by which human beings are remembered or forgotten. "Survival of the fittest" has been promulgated
as the great law of the universe. Of the innumerable multitude gone in countless ages "to the pale
realms of shade," only a few bright and shining lights
have escaped oblivion. Only those of great ability
or achievement, or associated by character or circum-
stance with great and vital events, have won remembrance. But when we apply this principle to recent
periods, and especially to our own field of observation, we are stumbled. We take, for instance, one of
our Connecticut towns, study its civil and church
records, exhume its lists of public functionaries in
every department, extract from living sources every
available item, and flatter ourselves that we have

[*] Read before Connecticut Historical Society.

gained exhaustive knowledge of every past resident
connected with its development, and then stumble by
chance upon some note-worthy personage who had
somehow slipped out of present remembrance.

"Why have you robbed me of a grandfather?" que-
ries an aggrieved descendant. After all our care we
are called to account for other vital omissions. *Is*
this "survival of the fittest" an universal law, as applied to those who have won or failed to win the boon
of permanent remembrance? Is it not quite possible that names are left out and forgotten as worthy
of remembrance as many that still survive in text-
book and history? In a modern and carefully prepared "Cyclopædia of American Biography" we find
many names once honored are missing. Froude has
given us interesting pictures of "Forgotten Worthies" in the mother country. May we not with equal
profit recall to memory some Connecticut worthies
once prominent but overlooked and in part forgotten.

James Fitch, Junior, of Norwich and Canterbury,
may be called in a certain sense the Father of Windham County, owning for a time the greater part of the
territory, selling the land and assisting in the organization of several townships. The oldest son of the
first, most honored minister of Norwich, son-in-law
of the worshipful Major John Mason, with much native shrewdness and force of character, no young
man in the colonies had a better start or more hope-

ful prospects. Very early in life he engaged in public
affairs, especially in relation to that very vital matter
in a new country—land surveys and transfers. In
military and political lines he was equally prominent,
attaining in a few years the rank of major and office
of county treasurer. Soon it appeared that he had
even exceeded his honored father and father-in-law
in influence over the Mohegan Indians, and had
gained control of a large part of their territory. The
drunken and flexible Owaneco—son of Uncas—in
1680 made over to his loving friend, James Fitch,
Jun., "the right and title to all his lands to dispose
of as he shall see cause," while the General Court of
Connecticut constituted him the legal guardian of
this Mohegan chieftain. The whole Wabbaquasset
country, a tract extending forty-five miles west of the
Quinebaug river and north as far as Massachusetts
would allow, was thus placed within his disposal and
practical ownership. But just as Major Fitch was
preparing to lay out this princely domain, negotia-
ting for the sale of the future Pomfret and Brooklyn,
he was compelled by the process of events, and the
administration of Sir Edmund Andros, to observe a
season of "innocuous desuetude." Fitch was far too
shrewd a man to waste time and money in attempting to secure confirmation of his land from that des-
potic ruler, in whose eyes an Indian deed was "worth
no more than the scratch of a bear's paw," but quietly

bided his time till that welcome Revolution which
overthrew the power of James II and his detested
governor-general. He immediately bestirred himself in the re-instatement of colonial government,
"travelling" it was said, "from Dan to Beersheba, to
incite the freemen, and summon a General Court."
"By whom was the Charter of the Government restored," sneeringly asks an enemy of Connecticut,
"but by James Fitch, Nathaniel Stanley, and such
like *private men ?*" A private man instrumental in
such a public service is surely worthy of grateful remembrance.

After the first general election Fitch appears as
member of the council, and thenceforth figures as the
most prominent and picturesque personage in eastern Connecticut—a magistrate and military leader,
as well as proprietor of a vast tract of country. Selling out townships as if they were farms, surveying
disputed lands and bounds, holding courts of inquiry,
deciding vexed questions, he makes what seems like
royal progresses through his domains, with his accompanying retinue of Indians, soldiers, and land-job-
bers. The jealous eye of a contemporary, who could
not "see cause to acknowledge Capt. James Fitch to
be Lord Proprietor of this Colony," enables us to see
what power and authority he was exercising at this
early stage of his career. A "Remonstrance," laid
before the General Court by many of his majesty's

loyal and dutiful subjects, sets forth—"That Captain Fitch has laid claim to our established inheritance by pretences of grants from Owaneco . . . has procured the Wabbaquasset, Mohegan, Quinebaug and a great part of the Pequod country from Owaneco and hath already sold out vast tracts of our land to some now in England, Rhode Island, and some to *privateers* as we have been informed. . . . Let any man give an example of any of the King's subjects in Europe or America since the times of William the Conqueror till to-day that ever engrost so much land as Captain Fitch hath done in this Colony which was before given and confirmed to other men under the great seal of England, and we cannot but declare and protest against these sales as illegal. We cannot but declare against Captain Fitch his being such a great land-pirate and selling so much of our land to strangers and hope the General Court and our people will consider how pernicious a man Mr. Fitch is to the rising generation, and what a scandal it is to this government and how gravaminous to many of the Queen's subjects that a person who makes it his business to sell the freemen's lands shall any longer continue in office in this Colony."

But however strong opposition and remonstrance, it had no effect upon the position of our monopolist during the wars known as King William's and Queen Anne's. His influence over the Indians made him a

1*

tower of strength throughout those stormy years—
Massachusetts was forced to call upon him to defend
her frontier, where the Wabbaquassets would not be
ordered but by virtue of authority from Connecticut.
His new plantation at Peags-com-suck—now Canterbury—was made the rendezvous of many a military
expedition—the scene of many a martial and legal
conflict.

As Indian wars ceased Major Fitch was called to
battle for his land titles. His first fight was with
the heirs of Gov. John Winthrop, who claimed the
Quinebaug country—now included in Plainfield and
Canterbury—by an earlier Indian grant than that of
Owaneco to Major Fitch. The General Court, loath
to excite the ire of such spirited and powerful combatants, delayed decision. Both claimants proceeded to
sell out farms and encourage settlement. A guerrilla
warfare ensued between the Winthrop and Fitch
settlers. Bounds and fences were removed; crops
raised by one faction seized and carried off by the
other; future respected citizens clinched and threw
hatchets. Gay youngsters from Norwich, known in
later years as sober magistrates and councilors, make
raids upon the Indian corn-fields; scout the Major's
writs, and run away from the arresting constables.
Our friend, the Major, figures conspicuously in all
this wrangling; now sitting in judgment, and then
arraigned as offender. Great meetings of Courts and

Commissioners were held at Peags-com-suck—meetings that brought in picturesque conjunction representatives of old and new Connecticut, high official dignitaries, governors, ministers, magistrates, lawyers; Owaneco in royal state, with surviving Pequots, Nipmucks, and Narragansetts. After much sifting of conflicting testimony, the right of ownership was confirmed to Major Fitch, with reservations allowed to the Winthrops and other claimants.

During the administration of Gov. Fitz John Winthrop Major Fitch served at the head of the Council, and was entrusted with the revision of the colonial laws and other important public services. He was a friend of education—the first layman in Connecticut to offer material aid to her infant college; a friend of religion, helping to build meeting-houses and sustain ministers in his several townships, even when laboring under church censure and suspension for excess in conviviality. Above all else he was a friend of the people; an advocate of popular rights, contending as strenuously for the privileges of the Lower House in the General Assembly as previously against the domination of Andros. Unwilling, however, "that any private prejudice should hinder public good," he did not hesitate to use his great political and personal influence to keep Saltonstall in power, though afterwards .tauntingly reminding him—"That had I let you out of my hands know

assuredly yourself and Mr. Christopher had been
next year at liberty."

The closing years of Major Fitch were embittered
by dissensions and pecuniary embarrassment. His
large landed possessions involved him in serious
complications. The great "Mohegan Land-case"
entailed endless expense and trouble. The Government of Connecticut challenged his claim to certain
townships, and, when he proceeded to make sales of
land and lay out allotments, Gov. Saltonstall issued
a public proclamation forbidding plantation work
therein. Suffering from gout and harassed by business perplexities, our Major was thrown into such a
tempest of rage as to lose all sense of propriety and
respect for Government, and, as if he were indeed
"Lord Proprietor of the Colony," he immediately
put forth a counter proclamation from "The Honored
James Fitch, proprietor of a certain tract of land,
east of Enfield," asserting his right to the land and
his sovereign contempt for "a kind of proclamation
lately come forth," and the authority that issued it.

This audacious proceeding called out an immediate
summons to appear before the Governor and Council
to answer "for its false and seditious expressions;"
but the culprit, lame with the gout, and unable to
ride, refused to obey in terms scarcely less insolent
than the original document. The matter rested until the succeeding session of the General Court, May,

1717, when it was ordered that a warrant be sent "to
.arrest the said Fitch and have him before the Assembly." But before its execution the impulsive
Major, probably relieved from gout, and returning
to his better judgment, sent a most humble confession of his fault, "being heartily sorry and con-
demning himself therefor," and asking forgiveness of
His Honor and the Honorable Assembly. Indeed,
Major Fitch seems to have been thoroughly frightened,
not knowing but that banishment or imprisonment
awaited him. The Upper House upon consideration
proposed to let him off by a £20 fine—"a slight
punishment for so high a misdemeanor," but the
Lower House, faithful to its champion, insisted "that
the full and ingenuous acknowledgement was sufficient," and obtained an unconditional discharge.

With this exciting episode the Major disappears
from public life, and after a few years was laid to
rest in Canterbury churchyard. A blackened stone,
overgrown with briars and sumacs, tells of "his usefulness in his military and in his magistracy to which
he was chosen and served successively to ye great
acceptation and advantage of his country, being a
gentleman of good parts and very forward to promote ye civil and religious interests of it. Died Nov.
10, 1727, aged 80 years."

And yet this gentleman, so active, so useful, so
prominently connected with public affairs, so master-

ful and picturesque in character and circumstances,
has passed almost out of memory, his name omitted
from our standard Biographical Cyclopœdia, his services in great measure forgotten even in the section
which he once owned and dominated.

As Major Fitch passed off the stage a young neighbor of his came into view, destined to even wider
prominence in public matters of a very different nature. The questions that vexed the soul of our bel-
ligerent major were to a good degree settled, or out-
grown. Indian wars had practically ceased, Indian
land titles had been made over to Government, the
Indians themselves were fast passing away. Many
questions of public polity had been settled. Some
supposed to be settled were to rise again with inten-
sified strife and bitterness. When Major Fitch as
chairman of the Council in 1708 expressed his "great
approbation" of the result reached by the reverend
ministers of the colony in council at Saybrook, and
assented to that "happy agreement" by which all the
churches of Connecticut were to be "united in doctrine, worship and discipline," and all troublesome religious questionings silenced forever, he little dreamed
that that young neighbor of his would strike such tell-
ing blows against that "happy agreement" and
church establishment.

Elisha Paine, Junior, like James Fitch, was early
called into prominence. Sprung from a leading fam-

ily, with superior advantages of education, he entered
upon the practice of law in his native town and was
universally recognized as "having the best sense of
anyone in those parts." But while in the prime of
life, with every prospect of high eminence in his profession and in public affairs, he was caught in the
vortex of "the Great Revival," and thenceforth the
current of his life was changed.

This remarkable religious movement swept with
great power through Windham County. The settlers
of these new towns had shared in the preceding spiritual apathy. With the many labors crowding upon
them in public and private affairs, they had gone forward "in settling the worship of God;" had built
their meeting-houses, provided home and support for
their minister, assisted in church organization. Their
meeting-houses were filled with hearers; their children duly presented in baptism. But the living faith,
the constant sense of divine presence and guidance
that had so characterized their Puritan ancestors,
was largely in abeyance. Under what was known as
"The Halfway Covenant," men without religious experience were in a certain sense connected with the
churches and lowered the standard of piety. But a
reflex tide was setting in. Spiritual men like Jonathan Edwards were considering the situation. Revival movements were reported from the Connecticut
Valley, and then tidings of the wonderful effects of

Whitfield's progress and preaching roused universal
expectation and questioning. This general sentiment
is best seen in the narrative lately brought to light
of Nathan Cole, a plain farmer of Kensington Parish
in the vicinity of Middletown. He writes:

"Now it pleased God to send Mr. Whitfield into
this land & my hearing of his preaching at Philadel-
phia like one of the old aposels & many thousands
flocking after him to hear ye Gospel and great numbers were converted to Christ, I felt the spirit of God
drawing me by conviction. I longed to see & hear
him & wished he would come this way & I soon heard
he was come to New York and the Jarsies & great
multitudes flocking after him under great concern for
their souls and many converted which brought on my
concern more & more, hoping soon to see him but
next I heard he was on Long Island & next at Boston & next at Northampton, and then one morning
all on a sudden about 8 or 9 o'clock, there came a
messenger & said Mr. Whitfield preached at Hartford
& Wethersfield yesterday & is to preach at Middletown this morning at 10 o'clock. I was in my field
at work. I dropt my tool that I had in my hand &
run home & run through my house & had my wife
get ready quick to go & hear Mr. Whitfield preach
at Middletown & ran to my pasture for my horse
with all my might fearing I should be too late
to hear him. I brought my horse home & soon

mounted & took my wife up & went forward as
fast as I thought ye horse could bear & when
my horse began to be out of breath I would
get down & put my wife on the saddle & bid her
ride as fast as she could & not stop or slak for
me except I bad her & so I would run until I was almost out of breath & then mount my horse again &
so I did several times to favor my horse. We improved every moment to get along as if we were fleeing for our lives, all this while fearing we should be
too late to hear ye sermon for we had twelve miles to
ride dubble in littel more than an hour & we went
round by the upper housen parish & when we came
within half a mile of ye road that comes down from
Hartford, Wethersfield & Stepney to Middletown on
high land I saw before me a cloud or fog rising, I
first thought off from ye Great River but as I came
nearer the road I heard a noise something like a low
rumbling thunder & I presently found it was the
rumbling of horses feet coming down the road, and
this cloud was a cloud of dust made by ye running
of horses feet, it arose some rods into the air over
the tops of the hills and trees & when I came within
about twenty rods of the road I could see men &
horses slipping along in the cloud like shadows and
when I came nearer it was like a stidy stream of
horses, & their riders, scarcely a horse more than his
length behind another, all of a lather and foam with

2

sweat, their breath rolling out of their nostrils, in a
cloud of dust every jump, every horse seemed to go
with all his might to carry his rider to hear the news
from Heaven to ye saving of their souls. It made
me tremble to see the sight how ye world was in a
struggle. I found a vacance between two horses to
slip in my horse & my wife said, 'Law, our clothes
will be all spoiled, see how they look'—for they was
so covered with dust they looked almost all of a color,
coats & hats & shirts & horses. We went down in
the stream. I heard no man speak a word all the
way, three miles, but every one pressing forward in
great haste & when we got down to the old meeting-
house there was a great multitude, it was said to be
3 or 4000 of people assembled together. We got off
from our horses & shook off ye dust & the ministers
was then coming to ye meeting-house. I turned &
looked toward the Great River & saw the ferry boats
running swift forward and backward bringing over
loads of people, ye ores rowed nimble & quick;
everything, men, horses and boats seemed to be
struggling for life : ye land & ye banks over ye river
lookt black with people and horses. All along the
twelve miles I see no man at work in his field but all
seemed to be gone. When I see Mr. Whitfield come
up upon the Scaffil he looked almost angelical, a
young slim slender youth before some thousands of
people & with a bold undaunted countenance. And
my hearing how God was with him everywhere as he

came along it solumnized my mind & put me in a
trembling fear before he began to preach for he
looked as if he was clothed with authority from the
great God & a sweet sollome Solemnity sat upon his
brow, and my hearing him preach gave me a heart
wound by God's blessing, my old foundation was
broken up and I saw that my righteousness would
not serve me." *

Such was the beginning of the "Great Awaken-
ing." The chronicles of those days read like a sup-
plementary chapter of the Book of Acts. Men with
flaming hearts and tongues went everywhere preaching the word, and what seemed like the veritable out-
pouring of the Holy Ghost fell upon their hearers.
The revival impulse was felt in all the churches.
"This religious concern did in many parishes run
swiftly through most of the families, and there was
scarce a sermon preached but was blessed to promote
the work."

Among the first in Windham county to be brought
into the spirit of the revival was our Canterbury
lawyer, Elisha Paine. Of a speculative turn of mind
and remarkably candid and catholic spirit, Elisha
Paine had always manifested great interest in religious questions and doctrines, "inquiring into all
the different worships of New England with their
principles and behaviour," and had sometimes feared

* This visit occurred Oct. 23, 1740. Some changes in spelling have been
made in copying from the original manuscript.

"that the true religion was not in the land." But
the living words of the great preacher wrought
powerfully upon his own heart, and he was led to
feel that however he might judge the religion of
others his own "was of no value." Yielding himself
to this new influence he received a new spiritual
baptism, and religion became to him the one thing
of importance in the land.   His brother Solomon,
his sister, Mrs. Josiah Cleveland, and her family, and
other leading families in Canterbury, were also par-
takers in the revival influence.

This town of Canterbury was at this time peculiarly
situated. It had been for sometime without a settled
pastor, and the brethren of the church had exercised
an unusual degree of liberty in administering its
affairs. Owing in some degree to the influence of
Major Fitch and his carelessness in admitting inhabitants—some *even* from Rhode Island as we remember—it had a strong radical element. The
"Platform" adopted at Saybrook for the "Permanent
establishment" of church discipline in Connecticut,
had given certain powers to ministers and ministerial
associations that had been formerly exercised by independent churches. The Canterbury church ob-
jected to this Platform, but did not formally manifest
dissent until after the revived interest in all matters
pertaining to religious worship. A committee was
then appointed—to search into the former constitu-

tion of the church and make return. Meantime they
went forward in their efforts to secure a minister,
and carried on revival meetings in somewhat independent fashion. The journal of John Cleveland, a
Yale student, while passing his vacation at home,
gives pleasant glimpses of the situation.

His father's house is "a little Bethel;" his parents,
brothers and sisters filled with great joy. They go
from house to house in all parts of the town, holding
"very live meetings." "April 7. A meeting in the
evening, many filled. 9. A meeting at grandmother
Paine's. Christians useful. 12. This night went down
into town. Mills preached. Had some of us a very
live meeting. 13. Talked with Uncle Solomon about
religion. He related his experience. This afternoon
Mills preached. His words seemed to have a very
great effect upon the audience. There was a great
stir indeed. 21. A meeting at Uncle Elisha Paine's.
My father relates his experience. Walk with Mr.
Bradford among the hills to pray. 26. Spent the
forenoon in the mill-house in prayer and reading the
Scriptures. In the afternoon Mills gave a funeral
discourse on Samuel Adams. The children of God
were very live at the funeral. A spirit of exhortation
was poured down upon them. Two persons were
struck unto conviction. 27. Exceeding full of the
spirit. People had a brave meeting. May 2. Mr.
Avery preached. Widow Spalding came out full of
2*

joy. 4. Mr. Mosely of Canada Parish preached.
Considerable stir. Some distressed and some rejoicing. This day old Chaffery was struck into convictions while Solomon Paine was exhorting him."

Great religious interest and activity are indicated
in this report, with a tendency to extravagance and
enthusiasm but no appearance of discord. It gives
a picture of Christian neighborhoods warmly engaged
in religious work, with friendly interchange of labor.
But in this same joyful month of May, 1742, legislation was in progress that wholly changed the aspect.
The great religious movement had its inevitable ac-
companiment of excesses and disorders. As in the
infant churches founded by the apostles there were
"swellings, tumults" and irregularities; as in the
days of the Protestant Reformation there were out-
breakings of ungovernable fanaticism, so the "Great
Revival" in America had its share of scandalous disorders.

Our mortal senses are too weak to bear the open
vision of things unseen. These vivid presentations
of the supernatural have a tendency to unsettle and
unbalance our earthly minds. The sections visited
with greatest power by the Revival were newly
settled and imperfectly civilized. Schools were few
and poor; religious services formal and lifeless. Was
it strange that people growing up amid such circumstances, with little to occupy their minds, when sud-

denly brought into contact with such eloquence of
exhortation and spiritual influence, should be carried
out of themselves? The spirit that seized many com-
munities seemed more like intoxication than inspira-
tion. Groans, shrieks, and other manifestations
abounded in their meetings; visions, trances, and
convulsions were common. The stated ministers of
the churches, who had at first welcomed the revival,
were alarmed by these outbreaks. The Legislature
of Connecticut, which had taken such pains to secure
the orderly administration of church worship and
discipline, was even more scandalized by these
breaches of order and decorum. A convention of
ministers and messengers was summoned to meet at
Guilford, with the hope that it might "issue in the
accommodation of divisions, settling peace, love and
charity and promoting the true interests of religion;
for which there seems to be so general a concern
among the people of this land." The good ministers,
each with their tale of excesses and disorders, smart-
ing under the severe criticisms of Whitfield and his
followers, could see but one remedy for these evils.
These abnormal experiences, faintings, convulsions,
visions, uproarious shrieking and groaning, were
usually manifested through the agency of the itiner-
ant preacher; those ignorant unlicensed exhorters
who had sprung up in the wake of Mr. Whitfield.
The Legislature of Connecticut in its great wisdom

had devised a perfect system of religious administration. Each town was organized as one or more
religious society or societies. Every inhabitant of
the town was an organic member of this society,
meeting-houses and orthodox, learned ministers had
been provided, and all that was needful for peace,
quiet, and the true interest of religion was for every
man with his family to attend worship in the town
meeting-house and pay his share of the rate. Sup-
pression of itinerants was the one remedy recommended. Untaught by all the lessons of church
history, the new wine in its first spirited fermentation was to be forced into very old and tight bottles.

Therefore, in May, 1742, the Assembly proceeded
to enact—that whereas divers ministers, some ordained and licensed, and also some who had no eccle-
siastical authority or standing, had taken upon them
to go into parishes under the care of other ministers
and exhort the people in matters of religion, which
practise had a tendency to make divisions and con-
tentions, and to destroy the ecclesiastic constitution
established by the laws of this government—therefore, if any ordained minister should preach in any
other parish than his own without the invitation of
the stated minister or authorities he should be deprived of provision made for his support; if any person not an ordained minister should presume to
preach or exhort without similar authority, for every

such offence he was to be arrested and bound over
for trial in the penal sum of £100 ; and if any for-
eigner, licensed or not, presume to preach in any
town of Connecticut without permission from recognized authority, he should be sent out of colony
bounds as a vagrant.

This remarkable expedient for promoting peace,
love, and Christian unity was at once put into execution. The inevitable results followed. The revival
element was at once arraigned against the Government. Social religious meetings like those described
in Canterbury had now become lawless and disorderly conventicles, liable to be interrupted by the
warrant of the constable. The attempted suppres-
sion of free speech in a time of high religious excitement greatly increased the existing evil. In Canterbury, where so much freedom had been exercised,
these restrictions were peculiarly irksome. Up to
this date there was no appearance of the slightest
doctrinal dereliction or difference. All that the Revivalists required, apparently, was the privilege of
hearing any ministers they fancied and pouring out
their own souls in familiar religious conference, and
in these very points they were debarred or greatly
restricted. In a very few months of this new dispen-
sation conditions had greatly changed. The " gentleman of veracity," even then fulfilling his mission,
thus writes to the Boston Gazette :

"*Dec.* 16, 1742. Canterbury is in worse confusion than ever. Their minister has left them, and they grow more noisy and boisterous so that they can get no minister to preach to them yet. Colonel Dyer exerted his authority among them on the Lord's Day, endeavoring to still them when many were exhorting and making a great hubbub, and ordered the constable to do his office, but they replied, ' Get thee behind me, Satan !' and the noise and tumult increased to such a degree, for above an hour, that the exhorter could not begin his exercise. Lawyer Paine has set up for a preacher . . . and makes it his business to go from house to house and town to town to gain proselytes to this new religion. Consequences are much feared."

Elisha Paine had indeed felt constrained to carry to others the word that had wrought so powerfully in his own soul, and during the summer had applied to the Windham County Association of ministers for license to preach. The ministers who examined him were of opinion "that he was qualified, and that it was his duty to preach the Gospel." But as condition for receiving license he must subscribe to the Saybrook Platform as the Ecclesiastic Constitution of Connecticut. Regularly ordained ministers were also debarred from preaching, except on conditions prescribed by this same Constitution and its amendments. Men's minds move quickly in such times of excitement. Elisha Paine had never been in sympathy with Saybrook Platform, believing it to exercise power not warranted by Scripture. It needed little reflection to satisfy him that his specific call to preach from the Great Head of the church conferred a more valid license than anything that could be granted by an unscriptural organization, and so he began preaching from house to house, and on from town to town. Passing into Woodstock, then held by Massachusetts, he held an afternoon religious service in the house of John Morse, and as he was peacefully singing the twenty-third Psalm he was arrested by a constable and carried before a justice. His conscience forbidding him to give bonds, he was taken to Worcester and closely confined "in the dirtiest prison that ever was seen." The imprisonment of a man of such high character and standing upon so trifling a charge, simply holding an afternoon religious meeting in a private house with a few neighbors, excited much talk and indignation, especially when it was found that such confinement was not warranted by the laws of Massachusetts. Many visited him in prison, and many petitions were sent for his release, and after holding him three months the authorities were fain to bid him depart, somewhat after the fashion of Paul's release from Philippi. Continuing his tour he was everywhere received with enthusiasm, his bonds falling out rather for the furtherance of the Revival movement.

In Canterbury, meantime, there was "confusion worse confounded," save that parties were becoming more clearly defined and antagonistic. The commit-

tee appointed to search into the constitution of the
church made return, Jan. 27, 1743 :

"That ye platform of church discipline, agreed upon by ye
Synod, at Cambridge, 1648, consisting of learned persons from
the four Colonies, is most agreeable to the former and designed
practice of this church (except their having ruling elders or distinct officers), and most agreeable to the Scriptures."

This report was accepted by a unanimous vote of
the church. No one pretended at this meeting that
the Saybrook Platform had ever been accepted by
the church, or was designed to govern it in future.
Even Colonel Dyer—the leading opposer to the Revival party—admitted that Cambridge Platform was
most agreeable to its "former and designed practice." The point of difference between the parties
was the power allowed by that Platform. Several
persons had brought letters of recommendation to
the Canterbury church, and were anxious to be admitted to its membership. The Revival party claimed
that in accordance with the ancient usage of Massachusetts churches they could receive such persons
into the church by vote of a majority of the members, in the absence of a pastor. It was therefore
put to vote :—

"That it is regular for this church to admit persons into this
church that are in full communion with other churches and come
regularly to this."

Colonel Dyer and Edward Raynsford protested earnestly against this vote as illegal and revolutionary, but it was carried by a clear majority. The right thus claimed was speedily exercised.

Ten brethren producing certificates from the pastors of divers churches that they were in full communion and regular standing with the same, the Canterbury church, in absence of a pastor, voted to receive them into its membership. Next the church proceeded to assert its right to take the initiative in the choice of a pastor. The controversy was becoming very lively. Ministers selected by either party were rejected with scorn and reprobation by the other. A majority of the church were pronounced Revivalists, but a majority of the society favored the opposition under the leadership of Col. Dyer, a prominent citizen who had control of the meeting-house and turned its key against Revival preachers. Orthodox ministers, on the other hand, were subjected to the most soul-searching inquisition as to their belief and experience. Both sides indulged in the vituperation common at that period. Col. Dyer called his opponents "sorry fellows," and ordered them "to hold their tongues." Meetings called for solemn prayer and fasting were made seasons of strife and debate. A formal complaint was laid against the proceedings of the church that they were taking this independent stand "to

3

make themselves strong, and were still fond of their
own wills." After much discussion as to the precise
nature of the fault committed by these complainants,
it was voted, " that they were guilty of evil surmis-
ings, irregular and unchristian treatment and disorderly behavior towards the church "—and, as they refused to explain or retract, a letter of admonition was
prepared and publicly administered. The difficulty
became so serious that public attention was called to
it. Through the advice and manipulations of several
worthy ministers on both sides of the controversy an
armistice was at length effected, the belligerents accepting reproofs and mediation from a composite
council, and consenting to hear on probation, as a
candidate for the vacant pastorate, Mr. James Cogswell of Lebanon, recommended by the ministers and
already approved by the society. And now for a
short time the people of Canterbury—Revivalists and
Conservatives, exhorters and society officers, met together in the well-filled meeting-house and submitted
to the ministrations of Mr. James Cogswell. He
was a Yale graduate of pleasing manners, amiable
temper and moderate opinions, and if tact and diplo-
macy could have healed the breach was just the man
to effect it. But not even an angel from heaven, as
Paul says, could satisfy parties in diametric opposition. In the violent fermentation accompanying the
Great Revival *new light* had been evolved which
proved a veritable x-ray in spiritual penetration.

Under this search-light, the half-way covenant allowed by the churches, and the domination of civil
authority in religious concerns, were seen in their
true inwardness as unwarranted by Scripture and
contrary to the practice of the early New England
churches. The arbitrary Act of 1742, restricting ministers to their own parishes, and silencing exhorters was especially obnoxious. Who placed a carnal
sword in the hands of Connecticut legislators? The
whole ecclesiastic system, devised and maintained
with such care by the leading ministers and laymen
of the colony, was condemned and renounced by ad-
vanced Revivalists, now know as "New Lights." A
thorough purification and sifting of the church, the
exclusion of half-way and dead members, and liberty to call and maintain a minister without the in-
tervention of civil authorities, was now demanded by
Elisha Paine and other progressive leaders in the
movement. That a conservative young minister,
however polished and logical his discourses, should
satisfy such hearers was simply impossible. Our
friend Elisha declared—"That he would rather be
burnt at the stake than hear such preaching," and
a large majority of the church shared in this judgment.

But the minority, worn out with the factious opposition of the Revivalists, now asserted itself. It was
useless to try to find a man that would suit both par-

ties. They liked Mr. Cogswell and were bound to
have him for pastor. And now the battle began in
earnest between a church minority backed by the
Government of Connecticut, and a New Light majority headed by Elisha Paine. The society proceeded
to call Mr. Cogswell to preach as a candidate; the
New Lights, conscientiously objecting " to spend the
precious day of the Lord under a general and lifeless preaching," formally withdrew from the stated
worship. A majority of the church voted, " To ap-
point the house of Samuel Wadsworth to be a place
to meet in by themselves to serve the Lord in spirit
and in truth,"—thus openly setting at naught the
law of the colony. Officers of the law were quick to
enforce the prescribed penalty. Elisha Paine and
Benajah Douglas, a zealous brother, were arrested
and hurried off to Windham jail on charge " of
preaching the Gospel of Jesus Christ," in a place not
recognized by the Constitution of Connecticut—and
without required license. The whole county was
stirred by these proceedings. Crowds of people
flocked to the jail, so eager to see and hear the prisoners that Paine was allowed to preach in the jail
yard by giving security. Indignant Conservatives
protested against this liberty, insisting that the sheriff
should be made to drive the people out and keep the
doors locked. Meanwhile the Ministerial Associations and high officials of the colony were encour-

aging and abetting the Canterbury minority in their
efforts to put down the New Lights and settle an
orthodox minister.

In September, 1744, the society proceeded to give
a formal " call " to Mr. Cogswell. The church immediately held a meeting, in which a large majority
protested against this call as an usurpation of power
delegated to the church alone. They also made a
formal proposition that, if those in church and society who chose to settle Mr. Cogswell as their pastor
and follow Saybrook Platform would allow the majority their share of the meeting-house they had
helped build, and free them from the charge of supporting Mr. Cogswell, they would oblige themselves
to keep up regular public worship, and refrain from
all further opposition to his settlement—but this
proposition, which seems to modern eyes so just and
reasonable, and all other protests and remonstrances
were scornfully rejected. To grant such privileges
to schismatic New Lights, open opposers of the church
establishment of Connecticut, was entirely out of the
question. The eyes of the whole colony were upon
Canterbury. No other church had taken so bold a
stand. Yale college was now dealing with our young
collegiate, John Cleaveland, and his brother, Ebenezer, who, during the summer vacation, had attended
the meetings at Mr. Wadsworth's house with their
parents, thereby transgressing the college law which

3*

forbade attendance upon irregular or separate meetings. The young men explained that they did not
know that this law was in force when they were out
of college in vacation, and had not supposed that
these meetings, held by a major vote of the church
to which they belonged, were to be considered unlawful or separate.

"A few more than half makes no difference," replied Rector Clap, as the meetings were held in a
private house, and conducted by unlicensed exhortors.
John Cleaveland then petitioned:

"To the Rev⁴. and Hon⁴. Rector and Tutors of Yale College
in New Haven. Rev⁴. & Hon⁴.

"It hath been a very great concern and trouble to me, that my
conduct in the late vacancy [vacation] has been such as not to
maintain interest in your favor, and still retain the great privileges that I have enjoyed for three years past under your learned,
wise, and faithful instruction and government. Nothing of an
outward nature can equally affect me with that of being hence-
forward wholly secluded from the same.

"Hon⁴. Fathers, suffer me to lie at your feet, and intreat your
compassionate forgiveness to an offending child wherein I have
transgressed.

Venerable Sirs: I entreat you, for your paternal wisdom and
clemency, to make in my case such kind allowance for the want
of that penetration and solid judgment expected in riper heads
—as tender parents are naturally disposed in respect of their
weak children. But more especially I beg to be admitted in
the humblest manner to suggest as a motive of your compassion
to the ignorant,—that I did not know it was a transgression of

either the Laws of God, this Colony, or the College, for me, as a member, and in covenant with a particular church, as is generally owned to be a church of Jesus Christ, to meet together with a major part of said church for social worship. And therefore do beg and intreat that my ignorance may be suffered to apologize. For in respect to that fact, which to riper heads may appear to be a real transgression, I can assure you, Ven^ble Sirs, that I have endeavored to keep and observe all the known laws and customs of College unblamably. And I hope I shall for the future be enabled so to do, if I may be restored to a standing again in my class. Thus begging your compassion, I subscribe, your humble servant and obedient pupil,

New Haven, Nov. 26, 1744.   JOHN CLEAVELAND."

But no plea of ignorance or appeal for mercy could condone such an offence. Nothing would satisfy the obdurate rector and faculty but a public confession in the hall, by the offenders, " That they had violated the laws of God, the Colony and the College." This confession the young students could not in conscience make, and after suitable space for reflection and re- pentance they were publicly expelled and commanded to depart the hall and college limits, never more to return. Likewise their fellow students were forbid- den to hold farther communication with them " lest they be infected thereby "—and all this because like good boys they had gone to church with their parents in vacation.

Their New Light friends of Canterbury, were at the same date receiving sentence. The Windham

County Consociation was convened December, 1744,
for the ordination of Mr. Cogswell. At a previous
meeting, attended by the whole church, a large majority refused to concur in this ordination, and denied
the authority of Saybrook Platform to coerce them.
Brethren who looked upon themselves as under Saybrook Regulations, sixteen in number, "did then move
to the east side of the meeting-house, chose a mod-
erator, and then, by a unanimous vote, concurred with
the society in calling Mr. James Cogswell to become
their pastor." Whether his ordination would be allowed under this minority call was a question that
excited much interest. An elect body of ministers
and delegates was to sit in judgment and decide. A
large assembly listened to their deliberations—all the
inhabitants of Canterbury and neighboring towns,
with many from distant sections—grave ministers
and magistrates, friends of law and order, and all the
more prominent New Lights and their sympathizers.
So great a gathering had probably not been wit-
nessed in Canterbury since the days of the Fitch and
Winthrop controversy, but how much more deep and
soul-stirring the interest now exhibited with such vital principles at stake. The facts of the case were
clearly set forth—the question deduced was very
simple—Is this body of sixteen Saybrook Platform
brethren *the* church of Canterbury ? In opposition it
was shown that the church at first had simply cove-

nanted to walk with God and one another, and had
supposed itself Congregational: that when it settled
its second pastor they made him sign with them an
explicit statement that they were under Cambridge
and not Saybrook Platform, and had still farther rejected Saybrook Platform by the unanimous vote of
1743. After prolonged examination and discussion
the council gave judgment—

That, according to the law of the colony and usage
in the churches, all churches within Connecticut government were supposed and understood to be under
Saybrook Platform Regulation unless, by formal vote,
covenant or agreement they manifested dissent as
such a body and in such church capacity ; that the
church of Canterbury, whatever its private sentiments
might have been, did not thus formally and publicly
manifest dissent before the vote of 1743, and that
those who on that day expressed their preference for
Cambridge Platform had thus denominated themselves another church, and *separated* themselves from
those who adhered to Saybrook Regulation, and that,
therefore, brethren now abiding in the above Regulation should thenceforward be recognized in law as
the church of Canterbury.

This decision, perhaps, marks the maximum of
Connecticut's attainment in her coalition of church
and State, placing Saybrook Platform as her ecclesiastic constitution upon the same footing virtually as

the state religions of the Old World. Its announcement at this juncture, strengthening the hands of the
ministry and government, was received with much
satisfaction by the friends of law and order. The
minority in Canterbury was greatly elated by its victory, and straightway installed the minister of their
choice with due ceremony and felicitations.

But the rejoicing was not wholly confined to the
victors. The defeated New Lights rejoiced in that
they were deemed worthy to suffer in behalf of their
principles. And, farther, they rejoiced in the divid-
ing line so clearly manifested; in the separation thus
avowed and promulgated between the New Lights
and their opposers—as "two different, distinct bodies, acting in two different kingdoms"—the one had
chosen "their glorious, exalted Redeemer to be their
only Head:" the other had chosen for its head an
unscriptural, human institution—the Constitution of
the colony. Many years later, Ebenezer Frothing-
ham of Middletown recalled to the memory of Canterbury Separates the raptures of "that blessed,
sweet and glorious day, when the first visible flock of
Christ in the Colony took up Christ's sweet cross to
follow the Lamb," with such gracious manifestations
of "Divine power and presence, and truth flowing in
a living stream from heart to heart." Not only did
the Separate movement throughout the colony receive a marvelous impulse by this decision, but it

served as the spoken word by which a certain definiteness of statement and aim was evolved from the previous chaos, and various conflicting elements brought to unite in determined hostility to the church establishment that claimed such supreme power.

The Canterbury Separate Church, as it was now called, though unstated in the eye of the law, robbed of its birthright, deprived of legal existence and privileges, could still rejoice in the heroic stand it had taken and the liberty it had achieved—liberty at least to choose a minister "after God's heart" and their own fancy, and order its worship after the Gospel pattern. As the first church in Connecticut, and probably in New England, of avowed New Light or Separate principles, it held a most conspicuous and influential position. With eagerness it embraced the earliest opportunity to re-affirm the original church covenant, and also to guard against things that might lead to "darkness and corruption" by making some points "more plain and particular," especially with regard to admitting into the church none but true believers assured of their own conversion, and the use of civil power in securing support of the minister. This amended covenant was signed at first by some sixty church members, and by many others in the course of a few months, representing some of the most substantial families of the town.

Renewing its attempt to call and settle a minister,

it first addressed its "dear and honored father," Elisha
Paine, but the leadings of Providence clearly calling
him to a wider field, it finally made choice of his
brother Solomon, who, after serious spiritual conflict,
accepted the call, and was formally ordained pastor of
the "First or regular Congregational church of Canterbury." This matter of ordination was accomplished with much difficulty—the established ministry of the colony disdainfully reprobating such
irregular proceedings—but relief was procured by
means of a Separate exhorter, Thomas Denison,
who had been regularly ordained by Rev. Ebenezer
Moulton, of Brimfield, a Baptist minister, who could
trace back in ministerial succession to three of the
most noted Puritan ministers of Boston. With his
assistance an attempt was made in Mansfield to ordain
their good brother and deacon, Thomas Marsh, as
teaching elder of the Separate church. But when a
great concourse of people gathered on the appointed
day to witness the services, they found that the good
deacon had been arrested the day previous on charge
of preaching the Gospel of Jesus Christ without lawful license or authority, and was "closely locked up"
in Windham jail. That the services carried on that
day in Mansfield by Elisha Paine and other Separate
leaders were highly inflammatory in character is not
surprising. Nor was the excitement lessened by the
appearance upon the scene of that most formidable

body—the Windham County Association—"fourteen
learned ministers," armed with all the powers and
terrors of ecclesiastic authority, hoping by this united
appearing and testimony to scatter the evil forces of
Separatism—attempting, says Backus, "to scatter
that flock after their shepherd was smitten." But the
storm evoked had passed far beyond human manipu-
lation. The ministers met a most tumultuous reception. Their attempted arguments and remonstrances
were drowned " in unchristian and approbrious revil-
ings," and they were forced to retreat, after reading
a formal protest in the name of the appointed ecclesiastic authority of the county. A month later the
Mansfield Separates succeeded in carrying through
the ordination of another brother, John Hovey, while
good Deacon Marsh was kept locked up in jail for six
months.

But despite, and partly because of, these very ob-
stacles and persecutions, Separatism was making
great advances. Not only in Connecticut but all
over New England, Christians were coming out from
the established churches. "Come out from among
them and be ye separate," was the cry that rang
through the land. " Come out from these dead and
corrupted churches; from the abominable tyranny of
those unchristian and ungodly Civil Constitutions,
and rejoice in the liberty wherewith Christ has made
us free." Every town, nearly every community, was

4

stirred by this religious movement; masses of enthusiastic Separates, breaking away from the yoke
of Egyptian bondage in joyful hope of establishing
a pure church and hastening forward the glorious
day of gospel grace and deliverance. Ignorant,
fanatical, unaccustomed to self or church government, burning with zeal and righteous indignation,
how great their need of wise and competent leadership.   One man alone, according to the church
historian, Rev. Isaac Backus, was equal to the occasion.   To one man above all others they turned
for help and guidance; Elisha Paine was the Moses
to lead the Separates from Egypt to the Promised
Land. From every quarter came to him letters and
messengers beseeching his presence and aid, and to
this work he dedicated his life and energies. Like
Wesley, of later times, he went about his mission,
traveling from town to town and from one colony to
another, everywhere aiding in the formation and
building up of Separate churches. His superior education and sound judgment enabled him in some
degree to direct and control the seething elements.
"A mixed multitude" accompanied the Israelites out
of Egypt. The Separate movement swept through
the lowest stratum of society, in a day of comparative ignorance and imperfect civilization, taking in
not only the ignorant, fanatical and visionary, cranks
of every variety, but the sore-heads, the grumbleto-

nians; all who for any cause were brought into opposition to constituted authorities. To bring these
scattered and disorderly congregations into anything
like coherent and orderly church estate, seemed a
task beyond the power of mortals. But Paine and
other devoted Separates went bravely forward, trusting in the righteousness of their cause and the help
of their divine Leader. The Mansfield Separate
church adopted and published an elaborate covenant,
which may be considered the official statement of
New Light doctrine and practice. A pure church,
perfect assurance of conversion and salvation in every
member, liberty to choose and set aside its own officers, and, also, to preach, exhort, and support the
preacher in its own fashion, were its distinguishing
characteristics. As far as possible this covenant was
made the standard in other Separate churches. The
destruction of Saybrook Platform was made a special
object in Connecticut. "A Short View of the Constitution of the Church of Christ," and the difference
between it and the church as established by Civil Authority, published by Solomon Paine, serving " as a
burning torch to enlighten the conscience" in this
regard. The views and practices of the several
churches depended much upon the character of their
leaders and the strength of the separation. In com-
munities like Canterbury and Plainfield, where it included a majority of the respectable families, they

differed little from other Congregational churches
except in greater spirituality and liberty of speech.
The testimony of Rev. David Rowland, pastor of the
standing church of Plainfield, who by reason of his
position was obnoxious to the New Lights, has great
weight.   He writes, at a later date—

" Although some things appeared among them at first very unwarrantable, yet considering their infant state it must be acknowledged by all that were acquainted with them, that they
were a people, in general, conscientiously engaged in promoting
truth, and Mr. Stevens, their minister, a very clear and powerful
preacher of the Gospel, as must be acknowledged by all who
heard him."

But while laboring " to guard against things that
might lead to darkness and corruption," they admitted one fatal error—the assumed possession of
the " key of knowledge," by which they not only had
perfect assurance of their own conversion and eternal salvation, but through " the inward actings of
their own souls " could test the spiritual condition of
all with whom they came in contact.   The adoption
of this pernicious principle wrought incalculable mis-
chief—leading the New Lights to despise human
knowledge, to set their own personal impression
against all evidence and authority, and above all to
deny the possession of true religion to Christians
whose experience varied from their standard.   It led

them to denounce with most scathing severity the.
ministry and membership of the established churches.
Nothing brought the Separates into such disrepute
with true friends of the Revival as the abuse and
maledictions poured out upon the standing churches.

But when turned upon themselves the use of this
supernatural key was even more disastrous. No one
was safe from the "inward acting" of his neighbor's
soul. Few of these perfectly assured and regener-
ated church members, escaped church censure and
discipline. Their records are filled with accusations,
trials, admonitions, and excommunications. With no
authority back of themselves to settle their disputes,
trusting to their own impulses and literal interpretation of detached passages of scripture, these loosely
organized bodies quickly fell into scandalous disorder
and confusion. Letters coming to Elisha Paine from
many New Light organizations show how widespread
were these difficulties and disorders.

And against these bodies of struggling Separates
were ranged all the forces of civil and ecclesiastic authority. To the Government of Connecticut the New
Lights were simply outlaws, excluded by special act
of legislation from privileges granted to other dis-
senting churches. Deluded Baptists and intruding
Episcopalians might claim the benefit of The Toleration Act, but for the rebellious children of their own
favored churches there could be no release or mercy.

4*

Did the New Light leaders, taunted with their own
ignorance, attempt to found an academy at New
London for the better instruction of young men as
Christian teachers and exhorters (an experimental
Northfield)? A law was at once enacted, October,
1742, forbidding the establishment of such school or
academy for young persons without liberty from the
Assembly, upon very severe penalties. Should such
unlawful school be established the civil authority of
a town was ordered to make inspection, and proceed
with such scholars and students, and such as harbor
or board them, according to the law of the colony respecting transient persons. In the same Act it provided—that no person that has not been graduated in
Yale or Harvard colleges, or other Protestant college,
shall take the benefit of the laws of the Government
respecting the settlement and estate of ministers.
And while thus denying New Lights liberty of speech
and worship, liberty to found and attend schools of
their own order, they took from them as far as possible every civil right. Separates were excluded from
town offices; men of substance and character, like
Obediah Johnson, of Canterbury, when elected representative to the Assembly by a majority of his fellow
citizens, was not allowed to take his seat because of
holding the office of deacon in the rebellious church.
Ordained Separate ministers were shut up in jail for
joining in marriage their own church members. Bap-

tisms and marriages performed by them were pronounced illegal. And worse than all in its effects,
touching all classes, were the rates extorted for the
support of the established churches. In the eyes of
the law each Separate was still a member of the parish
in which he resided, and obliged to pay for the support of its stated religious worship. Refusing to pay,
his goods were forcibly taken by the collector, and,
however much exceeding the amount due, no overplus
was ever returned. If goods were insufficient the men
were carried to prison. These were the days of Connecticut's "religious persecution," not bloody, indeed,
but most harrassing and persistent. All over the colony were heard the cries of these afflicted Separates—
men dragged to jail by force, wives and children left
helpless at home. Instances of special hardship are
noted—the poor man's only cow driven away from
his door, the meat or grain laid up for winter suste-
nance carried off by the merciless collector. Windham jail was so crowded with victims as to require an
additional story. In Norwich, where there was a
strong New Light element, the contest was very
bitter. The venerable mother of the church historian,
Rev. Isaac Backus, was taken from her home and
confined thirteen days in jail for refusing to pay her
church rate. It took the constable and six assistants
to carry a resistant brother to jail. Rev. Alexander
Miller, of Voluntown, ancestor of the late Hon.

William L. Gaston, of Massachusetts, tells his story
in the subjoined petition:

"Whereas, we are rendered incapable upon the account of
sickness and imprisonment, of sending a petition, we take this
opportunity of informing your Honors of the difficulties we
have met with as to our outward man because we are constrained
to observe and follow the dictates of our own conscience, agreeable to the Word of God, in matters of religion, looking upon it
to be God's prerogative to order the affairs of his own worship.
We are of that number who soberly dissented from the Church
established by Conn. and though we have no design to act in
contempt of any lawful authority, or to disturb any religious
society, but only to worship God according to the rules he has
given us in his Word in that way now called Separation, yet
have we suffered the loss of much of our goods, particularly because we could not in conscience pay minister's rates, it appearing to us very contrary to the way that the Lord hath ordained
even the present way in which ministry are maintained—Poor
men's estates taken away and sold for less than a quarter of their
value, and no overplus returned, as hath been the case of your
Honor's poor informers; yea, poor men's cows taken when they
had but one for the support of their families, and the children
crying for milk and could get none, because the collector had
taken their cow for minister's rates. Neither have they stopped
here, though we have never resisted them, but when our goods
could no longer suffice we were taken from our families and cast
into prison, where some of us have lain above two months, far
distant from our families, who are in very difficult circumstances.
Yea! and here we must unavoidably lie the remainder of our
days unless we consent to such methods for which we can see
no warrant in God's Word. No! surely it never came into his

mind, neither hath he commanded that it should be so, that the
Gospel of Peace should be so maintained ; he hath told his ministers how they shall have their maintenance, but not a word of
imprisoning men for refusing to maintain them, surely the best
things corrupted form the worst. And now, we pray you to
take notice of our difficulties, and grant us relief from bondage
that we may enjoy the privileges other dissenters enjoy.

Windham Prison, May 18, 1762."

No notice was taken of this representation, and the
prisoners were kept in jail till the authorities thought
proper to release them. Two years later they again
presented their case to the Assembly :—

· " We, whose names are subscribed, because we could not in
conscience pay minister's salary, which we find neither precept
nor example for in the Word of God, as we understand the same,
and after we had once and again suffered the loss of much of our
substance, being taken from us by collectors, our bodies were
taken . . . and cast into prison in said Windham jail, where
we were closely confined, some of us above twenty miles distant
from our families—where we lay some of us ten weeks in most
distressing circumstances as to our bodies, and our families reduced or exposed to difficulties too affecting to your Honors to
hear, could they be related. During which time we wrote to
you to inform you of our difficulties even while we were in
prison, but having been informed that said letter was never read
publicly and cannot be found, offer this to you.

ALEXANDER MILLER.
PETER MILLER.
JOSEPH SPALDING.
JOSEPH WARREN."

Elisha Paine, after the removal of his family to Long Island, returning in midwinter for household goods and stock, was arrested for rates due Mr. Cogswell and kept for months in Windham jail, to the great inconvenience and suffering of himself and family. Petitions sent to the General Assembly for relief in numberless cases were promptly " dismissed by both houses." A formal memorial presented in 1753, from the representatives of some twenty-five New Light churches, praying for the benefit of the Toleration Act, was scornfully rejected. Men whose hearts had been stirred in childhood by stories handed down from their grandfathers of the persecutions of. " Bloody Claver'ouse " and " Wicked Jeffries," now thrust their own brethren into like bondage. In vain was the parallel forced upon their notice—" We are but asking for the privileges for which our fathers bled and suffered and came to this new world."

" I can but marvel," says Elisha Paine, " to see how soon the children will forget the sword that drove their fathers into this land, and take hold of it as a jewel, and kill their grandchildren therewith." Again he writes—"The Roman Emperor was the first beast which persecuted the Christians that separated from their established religion, and by their law, fined, whipped, imprisoned and killed them ; we all own that the Pope or Papal throne is the Second Beast, which compels all under him to submit to his wor-

ship. Now what your prisoner requests of you is a
clear distinction between the Ecclesiastic Constitution of Connecticut, by which I am now held in prison,
and the aforesaid two thrones or beasts, in the foundation, constitution and support thereof." But their
eyes were blinded that they could not see distinction
or parallel. The mistakes, the excesses, the violence
and hostility of the Separates furnished, as was said,
" an awful specimen " of their need of this very system which they so bitterly denounced.

Failing in all attempts to procure relief from the
government of Connecticut, the Separates were driven
to appeal to the throne of Britain. Twenty Separate
churches prepared a memorial, praying King George
to grant them the benefit of the Toleration Act of
Great Britain. This memorial was carried to England by a special deputation in 1756, and first exhibited to the " Committee for the Dissenters." That
body received the report with amazement, and could
scarcely believe that the children of men who had
fled from the domination of a State religion would
have fashioned a parallel yoke for their own country-
men, and that Dissenters from the church establishment of Connecticut were denied privileges granted
to those in the mother country. This denial they
deemed a plain violation of charter rights and feared
that the presentation of the Separate memorial would
greatly injure Connecticut. The chairman's letter of

remonstrance and censure, and the disturbances accompanying the French and Indian war, modified
the policy of the government, and thenceforward exemption from rate paying under favorable circumstances, and other slight ameliorations of treatment,
was grudgingly accorded. But this leniency came
too late to save the great majority of Separates. A
number of their leaders were already gone, worn out
with the severity of the conflict; their churches had
wasted; the rank and file were greatly demoralized.
A few churches, indeed, struggled on, holding fast to
their peculiar principles, and in time secured a standing among the regular Congregational churches of
Connecticut, and are still represented by flourishing
and influential church fellowships. But for the great
mass it was defeat and bitter disappointment—their
buoyant hopes of a pure church and emancipation
from Saybrook yoke blasted and destroyed. Their
heroic stand for principle; their battle for eternal
rights and freedom degenerated into a noisy squab-
ble with rate collectors. The more substantial element went back into the stated churches; a very
respectable number allied themselves with the struggling Baptists; the remnant remaining were but Pa-
riahs and outcasts—"Wild Separates" as they were
called; veritable terrors; violent, factious, impracti-
cable, hurling anathemas upon all who disagreed
with them; their "hand against every man and every
man's hand against them."

To all outward appearance the "Separate movement" had failed completely. As a sect, as an organization, the New Lights were indeed "Spent Lights"
—*spent*, perhaps, but not wholly extinguished. Those
poor old Separates with all their faults, follies and
blunders, have indeed long since passed away—their
bodies resting in forgotten graves—but we rejoice to
believe that "their souls are marching on." The
principles for which they contended are now recognized and established; the liberty for which they
panted has become the birthright of every resident
of this great country; even that adamantine, inflexi-
ble *Platform* which they so battered and berated;
that Ecclesiastic Constitution of Connecticut so sacred in the eyes of our grandfathers, has been set
aside forever. And for these great and beneficent
results the Separates helped prepare the way, and
may be justly numbered with that "noble army of
martyrs" which through weary ages has borne aloft
the banner and shouted the battle-cry of religious
freedom. Those New Light doctrines and principles
that seemed at first so pernicious and revolutionary,
slowly working their way into Christian consciousness, became the prevailing theology of the succeeding generation. The familiar religious conference
and lay exhortation, which brought the Separates
fine and imprisonment, has long been recognized as
one of the most potent forces in the up-building and

strengthening of the church. And even "the ac-
cursed practise" of allowing women to speak in public, for which the Separates were severely reprobated,
is becoming a marvelous factor in the evangelization
and illumination of the world.

We have lost sight for a time of the chief leader in
this movement—the Canterbury lawyer, so active and
influential in its development. Unlike most of his
contemporaries, he lived to witness the apparent failure of his mission. As Separate churches died out
and his services were less demanded, he accepted the
pastorate of a New Light church at Bridgehampton,
L. I., and passed the evening of his days in quietly
administering to their needs. However great his disappointment, it made no change in his convictions or
temper. The faith that gave him such "sweet con-
tentment" when confined in jail for preaching the
Gospel he so much loved, kept his soul in perfect
peace. The diary of his former adversary, Rev.
James Cogswell, gives us a glimpse of him in his
farewell visit to his native town as late as 1769. He
sent for Mr. Cogswell to come and hear him preach
and returned his visit. They "discoursed in a friendly
manner." Mr. Cogswell took "the old gentleman"
to task for "meddling with Connecticut establishment" and "his notion of saving faith consisting in
assurance." Mr. Paine maintained his own views,
but "with a pleasant countenance," and temper free

from bitterness and severity.   A reformer without arrogance, a Separate without bigotry or uncharitableness, he stood far in advance of his generation, and the light of his teaching and example long lingered in Christian hearts.   Elisha Paine died in Bridgehampton in 1775, in his eighty-fourth year, having preached to his beloved flock till within fifteen days of his decease.

II.

WINDHAM COUNTY WOMEN OF OLDEN TIME.*

Our scant knowledge of early New England women is much to be regretted. While the deeds and lives of the Pilgrim fathers have been depicted for us in great variety of form, the Pilgrim mothers remain mostly in shadow. And as the sons of the first emigrants went out into the wilderness to build up other homes and settlements, the daughters are even more in abeyance. We learn by the self-sacrifice of Lady Arabella Johnson, the exquisite letters of Margaret Winthrop, something of the character and tone of those women who followed their husbands over the ocean. But of the great majority of those who helped build up thousands of homes in the waste places of New England we know comparatively nothing.

"Their name, their years, spelt by the unlettered muse," the date of birth, marriage, death, and birth of children, is all that has been left us. And yet we know that these mothers, wives, and daughters bore their full share in laying these foundations, and suffered even greater hardships and privations.

* Published in "The Plainfield Graphio."

The first woman within Windham county territory
of whom we know anything more than the above
data is Mrs. Abigail Bartholomew, second wife of
Samuel Paine. After the Woodstock colony had got-
ten in their first plantings of corn in the summer of
1686, they looked about for a miller, and invited William Bartholomew of Branford to fill this important
office. This stalwart pioneer had passed through a
number of exciting experiences, and while living in
Hatfield in 1677 had suffered the horrors of Indian
invasion, and saw his young daughter Abigail, then
five years old, carried away captive. The story of
capture, suffering, and escape was still fresh in memory, when, ten years later, she came with her father's
family to take up her abode in the plantation of New
Roxbury. It was the year after the close of King
Philip's war, when there was less thought of immediate danger. At about eleven o'clock in the morning
when most of the men were at work in the fields, the
savages burst in upon the settlement, killed twelve
persons, wounded five, set all the houses on fire, and
with seventeen prisoners, beat a hasty retreat. All
but five of the captives were women and children.
One man escaped to report their probable destruction.
All attempts at negotiation were foiled. The little
party was hurried on over the bleak country, up
rivers and lake, arriving at Canada in wintry weather,
They were the first New England captives who had

6*

been forced to travel through this dreary wilderness.
Two of the husbands of the captured women immediately bestirred themselves to procure their release.
Obtaining a commission from the government of
Massachusetts and tardy help from New York, they
toiled northward, mostly by water, carrying their
canoes upon their backs from Lake George to Lake
Champlain. On January 6, 1678, they reached Cham-
blee, and found the prisoners at Sorell and vicinity.
They then went on to Quebec, where they were civilly
entertained by the French Governor, terms of re-
demption agreed upon, and a guard allowed them to
Albany. On April 19 they started on their return
journey. Arriving at Albany May 22, they sent messages to those "loving friends and kindred at Hatfield," who for seven anxious months had wearily
waited for tidings :

"These few lines are to let you understand that we are arrived
at Albany now with the captives, and we now stand in need of
assistance, for my charges are very great and heavy ; and, therefore, any that have any love to our condition, let it move them
to come and help us in this strait. Three of the captives are
murdered, old goodman Plympton, Samuel Russell, Samuel
Foot's daughter. All the rest are alive and well, namely, Obadiah
Dickinson and his child, Mary Foot and her child, Hannah Jennings and three children, Abagail Allis, Abigail Bartholomew.
goodman Coleman's children, Samuel Kellogg, my wife and four
children, and Quintin Stockwell. I pray you hasten the matter,
for it requires great haste. Stay not for the Sabbath, not shoeing

of horses. We shall endeavor to meet you at Kinderhawk.
Bring provisions with you for us.

Your loving kinsman,

BENJAMIN WAITE."

As soon as possible a company was fitted out to
meet them as arranged. They rode through the
woods to Westfield and soon all reached home in
safety—the day of their arrival the most joyful day
that Hatfield had ever known. The ransom of the
captives cost about two hundred pounds, which was
gathered by contributions carried forward by "the
pious charity of the elders, ministers and congregations of the several towns." A daughter of Mrs.
Jennings, born in Canada, was named Captivity.

We may well believe that the presence in Woodstock of a young woman who had passed through
such an experience would excite great interest.
Indian alarms were frequent in those days. Again
and again the anxious inhabitants were forced to repair to the carefully-guarded garrisons. A trembling
fugitive, whose husband and children had been
butchered upon their own hearth-stone, brought the
news of the terrible massacre at Oxford. And all
through these troubled years our Abigail served as a
perpetual object lesson, showing to mothers and
children the reality of the peril that threatened them.
She married first, Joseph Frizzel, and later, Samuel
Paine, and lived to repeat to many children and

grandchildren the story of her marvelous captivity and escape.

Mrs. Esther Grosvenor, of Pomfret, comes down to us as a very distinct personality. Her husband, Mr. John Grosvenor, having died soon after completing negotiations for the Mashamoquet Purchase, Mrs. Grosvenor was much more concerned with business interests than most women of her day. Her name stands first upon the list of those receiving allotments of the Purchase, and she was naturally very prominent in division and distribution of the large estate. Born in England, she brought with her strength of constitution and dignity of character. A troublesome squaw once invaded her kitchen, demanding immediate supply of food, and even attempting to snatch the boiling meat from the kettle. Mrs. Grosvenor held her back with her broomstick till her son Ebenezer came to the rescue with more effective weapon. Like other women of superior station she was very helpful in care of the sick, and was viewed as a mother by the whole community. She retained to old age her vigor and habit of authority, and insisted upon walking to attend church service till within a short time of her decease.

In striking contrast with this "Colonial dame" is the first woman whose voice comes down to us from Brooklyn. A beautiful tract of land directly south of Mashamoquet was purchased by Sir John Blackwell in 1686, as agent in behalf of a number of English and Irish Dissenters, with expectation of founding a colony upon it. Capt. Blackwell also received from Connecticut a grant for a township, including his purchase, which was to be laid out as a separate town or manor, by the name of Mortlake. King William's accession in 1688, and the religious privileges now granted in Great Britain frustrated all these plans. Blackwell returned to England, and his purchase was left neglected till after his death in 1713 his son conveyed it to Jonathan Belcher, of Boston, who entrusted Capt. John Chandler, of Woodstock, with its survey and division. The tract was still in native wildness, save for one small clearing taken up by a squatter, Jabez Utter. To him Chandler granted at first a deed of the premises for his labor and expense " in building, fencing, clearing, breaking up, improving and subduing " the same. The probable reason why this bargain was not carried out, and for the non-appearance of Jabez in the subsequent expulsion is found in New London court records, wherein at just this date we find him arraigned for horse stealing, and sentenced to return the horse and pay the plaintiff ten pounds, also to pay the County Treasury forty shillings, or be whipped ten stripes on his naked body, etc.

Mary, the wife of Jabez, was a woman of spirit, and held on to her home with a woman's tenacity.

When the sheriff came to demand possession of the
premises, she barricaded doors and windows and
held on. All efforts failing to move her, young John
Chandler was sent to effect ejection. The story of
the siege is told by Mary herself in very vigorous
English. She gives the names of some twelve or fifteen young fellows from the neighboring towns who
aided in the raid, bringing with them drums, clubs,
axes, and all needful implements. Upon her utter
refusal to grant possession they proceeded to tear
down her fences, batter the house with stones and
clubs, set up ensigns of divers colors, drink to the
health of King James, committing, she says, "Many
high and heinous enormities, treasons, profanities,
and grievous wickedness." After carousing all day
they had an interval of quiet till towards morning,
when "they revived their noise, marching round the
house, beating drums, and singing psalm tunes," perhaps imitating the siege of Jericho, and then young
Chandler made proclamation: "Now we have got-
ten the victory; now the day is ours," and raising
poles against the house, three of the leaders vaulted
upon the roof, came down through the chimney,
opened the door and let in the sheriff. Even then
the resolute mistress refused to yield possession, and
had to be violently dragged out and flung down backward out of the door; but at last, late in the afternoon, " they drove me away from my home and drove

my children with me into the wilderness, and set a
guard about me, and left us there to perish without
any shelter but the Heavens,"—but still with life
enough to make her way to a justice, and make pitiful complaint as "his Majesty's distressed, forlorn
subject." Certainly no modern Brooklyn matron
could use her tongue more effectively than this first
woman resident.

Some pleasant glimpses of early home life in Windham county come to us from the diary of Mrs. Me-
hitabel Chandler Coit, of New London, whose husband, Thomas Coit, was brother of Plainfield's first
minister, Rev. Joseph Coit.

She writes :

"June 18, 1707. My husband and sister Sarah and I went to
Stonington, and brother Joseph Coit was married to Experience
Wheeler. June 21. We came home again."

Mrs. Coit was the sister of Capt. John Chandler,
of Woodstock, daughter of Dea. John Chandler.
When fifteen years of age she notes :

"May 31, 1688. My father, with his family, went to live att
New Roxbury, afterwards called Woodstock. Feb. 8, 1689.
Hannah Gary born, the first child that was born in Woodstock.
April 18. The Revolution at Boston. June 25, 1695. We were
married."

This diary was maintained through life, and while
noting prominent events, and the business ventures

of her husband—a pioneer ship-builder—it is mainly
taken up with domestic details, the birth of her six
children and childhood mishaps:

" June 14, 1706. Billy Colt fell into the cove and was almost
drownded. March 10, 1708. Martha Colt's foot burnt with a
warming pan. April 29. A plank fell off the stage upon Thomas
Colt and struck him down but gott no grate mater of hurt. Aug.
12. Mr. Vryland's vessell was burnt upon the stocks, and John
Colt's foot was burnt."

A visit at Woodstock in 1726 gives us a peep into
inside life ; those minor domestic details left out from
general history, and, therefore, all the more valuable :

" May 19. I set out to go to Woodstock, and before we got to
Bowlses it rained a smart shower and we fain to go in there for
shelter. When the shower was a little over we sat out again got
to Norwich, stayed at Lathrops that night and had fryed veal for
supper. Friday we dined at Cady's and had beef and pork and
herbs ; began to be very weary. I rid behind Sam Morris most of
the way ; got to W. a little before night, almost tired to death.
Sabbath day. Went to meeting ; come home very weary. 22.
Half dead still but went to brother Josephs a foot (just over the
line in Pomfret). 23. Came back again ; made seven calls on
the way and so to brothers very weary (Capt. John Chandler's,
South Woodstock). 24. Election day :—We went up to town ;
see trayning ; went to dinner at Coz. Johns, Billy and his wife
there too ; sister, cousin Hannah, Coz. Billy's wife and I called
at James Corbin's, Mr. Dwights, Jas. Bacons, Jabez Corbin's,
Dea. Morris's and Mr. Carpenters and so home ; same day coming home sister fell down and brake her arm ; they sent for Parker

(Dr. Morse) to set it. 25. Rainy weather; I went to Mrs. Holmes'; she is not married yet; at night Mr. Dwight and his wife and Mr. Morris here to see us; sister very bad with her arm. 26. A bright, charming morning; in the forenoon I read in the Turkish history; P. M., brother, Coz. Hannah and I went to Sam Morrises' (New Boston), had trout; to Coz. Billy's, and drank syllibub; came home very and dull; a pain in my face; I hate to ride; the horse started three or four times; I wisht to be at home 28. I went to meeting on foot; the text: "Happy are the people that are in such a case" (I could not think myself happy if I was in *his people's* case). 29. Brother John went with me to West Hill; we went to Marcy's, Paysons, Coy's and Wrights. 30. I set out to come home; brother Chandler came with me as far as change; brother Joseph came with me as far as Plainfield, there we met sister Abigail Coit; we went to dinner there, stayed an hour or two, then set out for Norwich; brother Coit came with us as far as Quinnebaugs; then we came over in a cannow; we sail over Shituckett alone; came to Norwich about dark; lodged at Lathrops. 31. Got home about 10 o'clock, not very wery; found all well except the garding, and this was overrun with weeds; so much for Woodstock."

To those familiar with the Woodstock of that date, this gives a very pleasant picture, naming all the old families and showing the neighborly intercourse that existed. Unpleasantness then rapidly culminating between Rev. Josiah Dwight and his people called out Mrs. Coit's disparaging comment. "Coz. John" was the youth who figured in the expulsion of Mary Utter. The wife of "Cousin Billy," then newly married, Jemima Bradbury, was a lineal descendant of

6

Massachusetts Winthrops and Dudleys, and one of
the most cultured women of her time, especially
noted for her interest in natural science.

Few lives have more of the element of tragic ro-
mance than that of the pioneer woman of South
Killingly, Mrs. Hannah (Wilson) Spalding. Her
husband, Jacob Spalding, of Plainfield, inherited a
right on the Owaneco Purchase, and was the first to
take possession of a Killingly section. His adven-
tures and exploits in connection with the Indians are
well known. Mrs. Spalding's prowess in routing a
noisy band attempting to force their way through the
window, by striking the leader on the mouth with an
enormous beef-bone, is handed down by admiring descendants. Jacob Spalding was killed instantly —
thrown from his cart on Black Hill—leaving his
widow and two children in comfortable circumstances.
Mrs. Spalding was an unusually attractive person, of
fine presence and character. To the great disgust of
friends and relatives she gave her hand in a few years
to an adventurer, who had figured among the Scotch
settlers of Voluntown, under the name of Girk. To
Mrs. Spalding he .confided that his real name was
Edward Stuart; that he was a lineal descendant of
the royal line, sharing the exile of the banished King.
His appearance and manners confirmed this story,
which was also vouched for by Rev. Samuel Dorrance
and other prominent settlers of Voluntown. Mr.

Dorrance performed the marriage ceremony, and
Edward Stuart reigned in the Spalding mansion.
There was much talk among the neighbors of his
fine clothes and lordly air. His linen was so fine
that it could be drawn through a ring; his gilded
rapier was of astonishing beauty and workmanship.
He spoke French with great fluency, and had great
skill in fencing. The only child of this marriage
was a daughter, named Mary in honor of the ill-fated
Queen. Soon after her birth, Stuart went abroad for
a year, in which he was supposed to have taken a
part in uprisings in England. After his return he
persuaded his wife to sell the farm she held in her
own right, and with the proceeds prepared for another
venture. His proceedings were at this time considered so suspicious that he was forbidden by the
town to harbor " one Sherrod," and for several days
before his final departure he maintained " a guarded
secrecy," and then stole away by night. From Balti-
more he wrote to his wife that he was about to make
one more effort to retrieve his fortunes and whatever
he might gain "it would not be too good to share
with her." This was the last ever heard of Edward
Stuart. The date of his disappearance tallies remarkably with that of the first concerted attempt by
Charles Edward to regain the throne of Britain.
Very extensive preparations had been made for this
invasion, but a great storm scattered the fleet and

wrought great destruction in life and property. If
Edward Stuart was what he claimed to be, he met
the fate of many of his associates.

Mrs. Stuart survived but a few months. Her health
had been greatly affected by the talk and suspicion
of her kindred and neighbors, and the estrangement
and opposition of her children. Mary Stuart grew
up a beautiful girl, strongly resembling her father in
manner and personal appearance, but the Stuart
destiny pursued her. The farm that would have
come to her having been pre-empted by her father,
she was forced through life to struggle with poverty.
Marrying when young, William Earl, of Brooklyn,
their home and its contents were destroyed by fire in
the middle of a winter night, the family barely es-
caping with their lives, wading barefoot through deep
snow. Hoping to repair this loss, Mr. Earl enlisted
in the unfortunate expedition to Havana, and died of
yellow fever. Mary supported herself and her two
sons till her marriage with a young carpenter, David
Dodge, and then enjoyed a few years of comparative
comfort and happiness. But with the Revolutionary
War new trials came. Her two Earl boys, fine,
spirited young men, were early induced to enlist, and
both died of exposure and disease. Mr. Dodge sunk
all his property in the manufacture of Continental
wagons ; Mary Stuart's health and nerves were completely shattered by all that she had passed through,

and her remaining days were clouded by sickness
and poverty. The children of her second marriage
were a comfort and support. Her daughter, Mrs.
Sprague, of Hampton, was a woman of unusual character and piety, and her son, David L. Dodge, after
a manly struggle, succeeding in founding that mer-
cantile house in New York, still represented by his
grandson, William E. Dodge.

Among the second generation of Windham women,
those born and reared within the county, none have
left a more precious record than Mary Whiting,
daughter of ·Rev. Samuel Whiting, of Windham.
Marrying the successor of her father in the ministry,
Rev. Thomas Clap, at the age of fifteen, she proved
more than equal to the position, lovely alike in person
and character. Her early death deepened the impression made by her. More than thirty years after
her decease, Dr. Daggett writes:

" She had a beautiful and pleasant countenance ; was a woman
of great prudence and discretion in the conduct of herself and
all her affairs ; was diligent, and always endeavored to make the
best of what she had ; the heart of her husband could safely
trust in her. She was kind and compassionate to the poor and
all in distress. She was adorned with an excellent spirit of
humility and meekness ; did not affect to put herself forward in
conversation, but chose to speak discreetly rather than much,
but was always free, pleasant and cheerful in conversation with
every one. She exceeded in a most serene, pleasant temper and
disposition of mind, which rendered her very agreeable to her

6*

husband and all her acquaintance ; and though he lived with her
almost nine years in the connubial state, yet he never once saw
her in any unpleasant temper, neither did one unpleasant word
pass between them on any occasion whatsoever."

The timeworn gravestone still bears record : " She
was of a most amiable disposition, the delight and
crown of her husband, an ornament to her sex and
pattern of every grace and virtue. She for a long
time expected death with a calmness and serenity of
mind, and met it with great joy and satisfaction. She
lived greatly desired, and died universally respected,
Aug. 10, 1736, in the 24th year of her age."

Many of the early women of Windham county far
exceeded modern practitioners in the extent and variety of their medical practice, though experience
with them took the place of training and diploma.
Mrs. Hannah Bradford, of Windham, was one always
ready to meet the call of sickness and suffering.
The Mrs. Holmes (of Woodstock) whom Mrs. Coit
reports as " not married yet," did in time select for
her second husband Mr. Edmonds of Dudley. Previous to this marriage she had devoted herself to
nursing, and it is said that in " the great snowstorm "
of 1749 her services were in such demand that she
was taken out of a chamber window and carried
through the drifts many miles to distressed patients.

Another woman very widely known as midwife,
nurse and physician, was Mrs Anne (Woodcock) Ea-

ton of Ashford, whose practice rivalled in extent the
most popular physicians of our day. It is said that
during the prevalence of a spotted fever she was
scarcely off her rounds, day or night, riding up occa-
sionally to her own doorstep, inquiring for the health
of her own family, snatching a bit of food and hurrying off again.

During the "Great Revival" of 1740, women came
decidedly to the front in the separation from the
stated churches. Their varied and incisive excuses
for refusing to attend worship at the town meeting-
house and withdrawal from church, show great fer-
tility of invention as well as devotion to principle.
Some of them even went such lengths as to indulge
in what was called by a Separate brother "the
cussed practice of women speaking in public."

Probably no woman in the county was so widely
known in her day as Mercy Wheeler of Plainfield, in
connection with her very remarkable "faith cure."
Few cases of this kind are so well attested, or reported with such *minutiæ* of process. She was a
respectable young woman of good family, and her
disabled and suffering condition was perfectly well
known to the townspeople. For a number of years
she seemed to have lost the use of the lower part of
her body—her ankle bones "loose and separate so
that a string was needful to keep her feet in proper
position," and the power of speech had been at times

taken from her. Her mind during this period had
remained clear and tranquil and especially open to
religious impressions. The revival of religion, for
which she had longed and prayed, was a source of
great joy to her. Hearing of the wonderful things
done throughout the land she queried in her own
mind whether the Lord would not send deliverance
to her, and awaited a meeting to be held in her own
house, with trembling hope. But when, after the
services of prayer and preaching no change came, a
cloud of darkness came over her till the word of
God came to her with such force—"If thou wilt believe thou shalt see the glory of God *now*"—that she
seemed to go out of herself and all human agency,
into the hands of God alone. At that instant a thrill
passed through her frame—"a racking, a working in
every joint, as if she were with hands drawn and com-
pressed together," and then to the utter amazement
of minister and people, who had known nothing of
the exercises of her mind, the bedridden woman, who
for sixteen years had not stood upon her feet, walked
up and down the room, crying "Bless the Lord Jesus
who has healed me."

The cure so suddenly effected was permanent.
Hundreds of people who had seen the crippled in-
valid now testified to the completeness of her cure.
The next Sabbath she rode three miles to the house
of worship, and thenceforth was able to engage in all

the ordinary duties of life. This wonderful story made a great impression at the time throughout the Colony. Dr. Benjamin Lord, of Norwich, was especially interested in the case and published his sermon preached at a special service of thanksgiving held in Plainfield, with affidavits from well-known residents as to Mercy's previous and present condition. This pamphlet passed through several editions and was widely circulated at home and abroad, even exciting interest and attention among Christians in England. All this notice and notoriety had no effect upon the simple, humble-minded Mercy, who proved the reality of her religion by faithful performance of everyday duties—"a living example of faith, fortitude, love, and unshaken constancy in religion."

These are specimens of those early women residents of Windham county whose names and acts have come down to us. Many more equally worthy of notice are lost to sight and memory.

III.

OTHER LIGHTS.

In connection with the revolutionary struggle
Windham county men came into prominence in council and field, whose names are enshrined among those
which the nation delighteth to honor. Our Trum-
bulls, Putnam, Knowlton, Grosvenors, McClellan, and
many lesser lights, are held in grateful remembrance
as those who bore a most honorable and helpful part
in establishing our national independence. But during this same period there were others, useful and
honored in their own callings, whose names have
passed into oblivion.

A very conspicuous instance of this failure to gain
a place in history and remembrance of one very
noted in his own generation, is that of Rev. Joseph
Howe, the beloved and popular pastor of New South
Church, Boston, 1773-1775. One letter of his that
has come down to us gives us a vivid picture of Boston under the administration of the famous Port Bill:

"Aug. 2, 1774. Boston it is true is a very different place in
some respects from what it was when you were here last. Then
trade flourished ; our harbor was whitened with canvass ; our
wharves and quays resembled a forest—a forest I mean of masts

and sail-yards ; and our common, that beautiful lawn to the west, was made more beautiful by the people that walked, and the herds that fed on it. But now to see our harbor and our common—how different ! In the former nothing is seen but armed ships ; in the latter but armed men. . . . It is true we have not yet felt the force of either the one or the other, and I pray God we never may. But yet to be threatened with it—to be insulted in various ways of a more private nature ; to have four regiments of troops in the heart of a large town ; to have all these evils brought upon us for our laudable and virtuous struggles in behalf of our just rights and liberties—is certainly to a mind of the least feeling, irritating and painful. And were you to come to Boston, I make no doubt that on these accounts your visit must be somewhat disagreeable to you.

However, in another view, these very evils would be the means of affording you pleasure ; while you saw with what calmness, with what patience, with what fortitude and firmness, with what persevering prudence and spirit the people endure them. And when I say the people, I say all but a few, a very few, and a particular class of men. It is not true that we are much divided. The Tories made their grand push about a month ago. And what was the effect of it ? Only to convince them and us that their whole number consisted of only about one hundred and twenty persons, inclusive of some who have since retracted. The Bostonians acquire courage every day. How can it be otherwise, when all the Continent are pitying and supporting them, and, above all, when we have that God to go to who heard our fathers when they cried unto Him, and who we trust will hear us also, their immediate descendants."

Joseph Howe, son of Rev. Perley and Damaris (Cady) Howe, was born in Killingly, Conn., 1747,

fitted for college by his step-father, Rev. Aaron
Brown; was graduated from Yale 1765 as the vale-
dictorian of an exceptionally able class. His townsman, Manasseh Cutler, the father of the "North
West Ordinance," Theodore Sedgwick, Berkshire
county, Mass., judge and United States Senator, and
many lesser lights, were included in this famous class.
Not one of them made his mark in the world so early
as Joseph Howe. First as teacher of the public
school at Hartford, then the most important educational institution of the kind in Connecticut, he won
immediate success and popularity. Accepting a
tutorship at Yale College, "his literary accomplishments, especially his remarkable powers of elocution,
not less than his fine social and moral qualities, rendered him a general favorite." Through his instruc-
tions the standard of public speaking and familiarity
with polite literature in the college was very considerably elevated, and to say of a successor that he
was "like Tutor Howe," was the maximum of praise.
Though frail in body he pursued theological studies
during his tutorship, and prepared to enter into the
ministry. His oratorical powers brought him at once
into notice—his exercises in the pulpit as reported by
admirers were of "the most impressive and fascinating kind." Wherever he went hearts, homes, and
pulpits were open to receive him. He received calls
to settlement from the leading churches of Connecti-

cut, in Hartford, Norwich, and Wethersfield. Visiting Boston for his health, he preached at the New
South Church, and was invited to become its pastor
upon one day's hearing—the church giving as its
ground for such phenomenal indiscretion—" the character which Mr. Howe had received from the voice of
mankind." After a year's delay Mr. Howe was
ordained pastor of this church May 19, 1773, President Daggett of Yale College preaching the sermon,
Dr. Chauncey of the First Church, Boston, giving
the right hand of fellowship. In this brief pastorate
Mr. Howe fully sustained his high reputation. The
magnetic charm of his address was at once recognized. He was the idol of the hour, the popular
preacher. The local rhymster sings :

> " At New South now, we'll visit Howe,
>   A Genius it is said, Sir ;
>   And here we'll hail, this son of Yale ;
>   There's not a wiser head, Sir.
>   May his fame soar like one of yore
>   Who Cromwell's court did grace
>   A better man, we trow, he can
>   See Lord's day face to face."

A Boston blue-stocking reports :

> " He in refined, pathetic sermons shone ;
>   His diction pure, his methods all his own ;
>   While his melodious voice his audience blest
>   And roused each noble passion in the breast."

7

According to Dr. Sprague his mind was "fitted
perhaps alike for rigid and profound investigation on
the one hand, and for the imaginative and rhetorical
on the other." And when to other merits was added
apparent unconsciousness of his great attractions and
an unusually liberal and catholic spirit, it is not
strange that he inspired enthusiastic attachment.

The breaking out of open hostilities closed the
churches of Boston and this successful ministry.
Worn out with labor and excitement, Mr. Howe returned to his old home in Connecticut, and after visiting his friends, succumbed to complicated disease,
dying in Hartford, August 25, 1775, at the house of Rev.
Elnathan Whitman, whose daughter, Elisabeth, he expected to marry. Amid all the stirring events of that
anxious summer his death made a deep impression
throughout New England. An elegy composed by
his Boston admirer depicts in deepest shades the
funeral solemnities :

> "The fair Eliza's anguish who can paint,
> Placed near the corse of our ascended saint :
> Though his blest soul ascends the upper skies
> Her gentle bosom heaves with tender sighs."

The obituary notice in the "Hartford Courant,"
after the extravagantly eulogistic fashion of the time,
enshrines Mr. Howe among the lights and benefactors of the world, the beauty of whose mind was

without a parallel; whose life was a treatise of ethics
and theology; a great and universal genuis. By the
generation that had honored him his memory was
fondly cherished, and years after his decease he was
again recalled to notice as the model hero in the first
pages of the "Life and Letters of Eliza Wharton."

And after all these eulogies he was forgotten!

"His leaf had perished in the green."

No reporter was there to note down even a frag-
ment of those thrilling discourses. No one paused
in those busy years to compile even a brief biography of the popular favorite, and so he slipped from
sight and memory. In our modern standard "Cyclopædia," of America Biography, of those bearing the
honored name of Fitch there are fourteen notices,
but never a "Major James" among them. There
are Paines, small and great, of almost endless number and variety, but no Rev. Elisha; and from the
brilliant array of Howes our Joseph is excluded, and
by a remarkable fatality his burial place at Hartford
is unmarked and unknown.

Quickly occurring losses were in part the cause of
this omission. His step-father died on the way back
from his funeral, and the bereaved wife and mother
soon followed, and amid the pressure and burdens
of Revolutionary years the brother's grave was
overlooked. Sketches in "Yale Biographies" and

"Sprague's Annals of the American Pulpit," and the obituary notices in "The Hartford Courant," comprise the most that can be learned of one who held so high a place among his contemporaries, perhaps the most brilliant young man of his generation.

In reviewing the life of Joseph Howe we are struck with the praise accorded to the fine manners and gracious bearing of this young minister and their influence upon his career. Even higher praise was called out in the case of his townsman and classmate, Manasseh Cutler, whose success in winning the favor and votes of southern chivalry for his immortal Ordinance was largely attributed to their admiration for his agreeable manners, excelling any previous specimens from New England. It is certainly remarkable that this rough old border-town of Killingly, with its wrangles and church feuds, should send out such gracious and elegant young men. Were these fine manners a heritage from distant ancestry, a residuum of that rare old English polish brought over by the better class of our first settlers, and taking on even a brighter lustre in the changed conditions of the new world? Class distinctions, as we know, were very strongly marked in the old colonial days. The common people were very common, rude and boorish in speech and manner. So much the more necessity that the upper class, those allied however remotely with noble families at home, should

hold tenaciously inherited, social traditions, and keep
aloof from those of lower social grade and rougher
manners. We fancy that the application of these
traditions was largely due to woman.

It is a common complaint that we see so little of
the mothers, wives, and sisters of our ante-revolution
fathers, but none the less were they a power behind
the throne. With little outside to occupy or distract
them they could consecrate their time and energies
to the care of their households. And while the men
were out in the world building up towns and institutions, these insulated women were impressing themselves upon the minds of their children, and so training them that they were fitted in turn to bear their
part in shaping the institutions of the new republic.
How the character of these unseen, unobtrusive
women shines out in their sons. From Washington downward, it would seem that every man prominently connected with the American Revolution and
establishment of Federal Government was favored
with a mother of superior excellence and intelligence.
We have the privilege to-day of intimate acquaintance with such noble specimens of womanhood as
Abigail Adams and Mercy Warren. We have the
letter written by Lydia (Dyer) Gray to her son at
Boston after the battle of Bunker Hill. And we
know there were many others equally alive to the
situation and wise in counsel. Here in Windham
7*

county we had Rachel McClellan planting "trees of
Liberty" on Woodstock common, and the wife of
Dr. David Holmes, held in such high respect for
"excellence of character and noble bearing." Still
earlier we hear the praises of the mother of Manasseh Cutler " adding to beauty and strength of mind,
an education in advance of her time." And while
no special record comes down to us of the mother of
Joseph Howe, we know that from her position as the
wife of ministers and daughter of one of the found-
ers of Pomfret library, that she must have ranked
among the cultured gentry, the true nobility of early
New England.

Across the Quinebaug in the neighboring town of
Pomfret, contemporary with Howe and Cutler, a
young man grew up who attained eminence in early
life and whose name and memory are still held in
honor, but who failed to gain credit for what in his
life's work he valued most. A descendant of the old
Waldensian stock, bearing the honored name of Albigence Waldo, he enjoyed the usual advantages of
education, pursuing general studies under his minister, Rev Aaron Putnam, and medical studies under
the most noted physician of the county, Dr. Elisha
Perkins of Plainfield. Entering into practice in his
native town, he won immediate success and popularity. But the critical condition of public affairs absorbed much time and energy. He served as clerk

to McClellan's famous " troop of horse " and upon
the first news of the battle at Lexington " he joined
his neighbors and marched to Cambridge where he
tarried till they came home together." He soon returned to the field as assistant surgeon of Col. Jedidiah Huntington's regiment, and for four years succeeding continued almost constantly in service. His
inoculation for and treatment of small-pox at Mon-
mouth and Valley Forge, " gained him much reputation," and the journals kept by him throw much light
upon the condition of the army. The demoralized currency—" three months wages barely paying a thirty
shilling debt "—and the suffering condition of his
family—" on the point of famishing with mere want
of food and every other necessary "—compelled Dr.
Waldo in 1779 to resign his position in the army and
resume his medical practice in Pomfret.

The valuable experience gained in army practice
with his native quickness and dexterity, placed Dr.
Waldo at the head of his profession in northeastern
Connecticut, especially in surgical practice. He became at once the popular physician of the day, his
services in constant demand over a large section of
country. His wide popularity is indicated by one
unfailing test—the number of children named for
him, rivaling those of any prominent presidential
candidate or successful military leader. But with
this flush of practice he was able to carry on exten-

sive investigations, not only in his own profession,
but in those varied scientific questionings then exciting so much interest. An associate for a time with
Dr. Elisha Perkins, the famous inventor of the " Me-
tallic Tractors," he shared his interest in the theory
of magnetic and electric currents, experimenting in
those mysterious agencies. His quick mind perceived
the benefits that might accrue from professional and
scientific association, and he promoted and carried
out a monthly meeting of the physicians in Windham
county as early as 1786. A formal county Medical
Society was formed in 1791, Dr. Albigence Waldo,
clerk, and in the following year he assisted in the
organization of the State Medical Society.

   With this extensive professional practice and scientific investigations, Dr. Waldo retained his interest
in all the living questions of the day, and was ever
ready to bear his part in all public and social enterprises. His literary accomplishment and fluency of
speech were highly esteemed, and he was called to
take a prominent part on many important occasions.
Among thousands of brother Masons he was selected
to pronounce the eulogy on behalf of the Masonic
order at the grave of Gen. Putnam, and he was accredited with valuable aid in the preparation of
Humphrey's " Life of Putnam." His literary aspirations and pursuits were shared by his second wife,
Lucy Cargill. She was the daughter of Capt. Benja-

min Cargill, a shrewd and genial Scotchman, proprietor of the Quinebaug mill privilege (now embraced
in Putnam city), a very noted and influential personage. He had a patriarchal family, whose names he
delighted to jingle in rhyme something in the style
of the late Hutchinson family, viz.:

> " Here's my good health to children dear,
> All in a row they jine
> Collected here, from far and near;
> And, lo, they are called mine.
>
> Here's William, Lucy, Asenath, too,
> And Ben, and Rhoda, five:
> Here's Phila, Ithael, Sall and Poll.
> And James and Charles, alive.
>
> And here are two adopted ones,
> I love you as the rest,
> And pray the Lord to smile on you
> And evermore be blest.
>
> And two are dead, I hope at rest,
> You living ones I call,
> And pray the Lord to smile on you
> And ever bless you all."

Mrs. Waldo's literary style was very unlike that of
her straightforward, Methodist father, being fashioned
after the sentimental Johnsonian then in vogue. It
was she who declined an invitation to a supper because of the illness of " her babe, that tender blossom,"

and her hand is evident in the epitaph upon a Revolutionary soldier, " who having worn his life out in
the service of his country, had gone to wave the Palm
of eternal Peace." But in spite of these little man-
nerisms she was a woman of good intellect, and held
with her husband a leading position in the best society of the day. This happy and triumphant period
of her life had but a short continuance. Dr. Waldo
died suddenly in 1794, in the prime of life and height
of professional eminence. Few deaths excite a wider
sympathy or leave a deeper void. He was borne to
the grave by members of the medical society, accompanied by the Masonic brethren and a great concourse
of weeping friends and admirers. Newspapers winged
his praises all over the land as " endowed by the God
of nature with the most brilliant and distinguished
abilities, and with a heart susceptible of all those
amiable and benevolent virtues which adorn the
human breast;" as one who "ranked among the
highest order of his profession, whose manuscripts
will doubtless afford great light and benefit to future
ages; who lived without an enemy, and died greatly
lamented by all." A suitable monument erected by
his fellow Masons testified to "their esteem and respect for the virtues, talents, and usefulness of their
late worthy brother . . . . who attentively studying
the works of God in the admirable frame of man rose
to eminent distinction in the noble art of healing;

his name was Charity; his actions, Humanity; his intercourse with men, Benevolence and Love. Born 1750; died 1794."

And after all this public manifestation of grief and adulation came a long and wearisome struggle for permanent recognition. Dr. Waldo, like the later Agassiz, had been too much absorbed in professional and scientific labors to care for making money; too busy, indeed, to collect what he had honestly earned. His accounts had been poorly kept and were found very difficult of collection, so that with all his extensive practice and high reputation, very little was left for the support of his family. And just at this juncture the Cargill establishment was broken up and scattered. The remarkable manner in which a family after a long course of unbroken prosperity and apparently fixed stability suddenly falls to pieces, was again signally illustrated. Three sons died in rapid succession, the old captain's health gave way, his property greatly depreciated in value. Mrs. Waldo, even more Johnsonian in affliction, thus writes to the widow of her brother, William Cargill:

"My father's baleful destiny reserved him the mournful spectacle of his dying eldest son, and who can express his affliction? His weeping eyes are as the dropping clouds; his melting breast as the thunder storm—clouds which break not away; a tempest without knowledge of a calm. What is left of life seems unsupportable and is not really life but a lingering death."

Giving up their pleasant home in the Quinebaug valley—the old "Cargill's Mills" where they had enjoyed so much happiness and prosperity, the old people passed the remainder of their lives alternating among the homes of the surviving children, under the especial care of Mrs. Waldo. But whatever other duties claimed her time and thought she steadfastly pursued one great aim—to bring the knowledge of her husband's scientific researches to the world and secure public recognition of his services. Herself destitute of means for publication she was compelled to ask aid of others, visiting and appealing to monied men in different parts of the land. Her letters—beautiful, pathetic, Johnsonian letters, with carefully hoarded copies at home—were sent to many distinguished parties. As tenderly and persistently as Evangeline sought her lost lover, so did Lucy Waldo seek the perpetuation of those memorials of her lost love—those precious manuscripts that were "to afford great light and benefit to future ages." How great their real value it is impossible now to estimate. Many things were lying round waiting to be discovered. Dr. Waldo had native quickness and keen insight, and his researches were in the line of those electric and magnetic forces that have transformed the world, and may have predated modern discoveries, but whether they did or not they were allowed to pass unnoticed. Again and again

Mrs. Waldo seemed about to attain her object; encouragement would be given; hopes raised; once a movement for publication was actually started; and then some obstacle would arise. Years passed on in reiterated effort and disappointment. The "tender blossom" drooped and faded; the old captain and his wife passed away; a pupil of Dr. Waldo's, Dr. Thomas Hubbard, filled his place at Pomfret, and even surpassed the fame of his teacher: little "Albes" and "Waldos," grown up into manhood, scoffed at the odd name given them in honor of an old time doctor.

> "Thousands of times has the same tale been told ;
> The world belongs to those who come the last."

But still the faithful wife carried her precious treasures from East to West, from one great man to another.

> "Fair was she and young when in hope began the long journey ;
> Faded was she and old, when in disappointment it ended."

Her last appeal was to Dr. Waldo's early friend and neighbor, Rev. Manasseh Cutler, D. D. "Carefully copied, illustrated with well executed drawings" the manuscripts were placed in his hands, "but for want of means the enterprise was again defeated," and Dr. Waldo's valued papers never saw the light.

Mrs. Waldo passed her declining years with a sister, and we may hope that the consciousness of hav-

8

ing done all within her power to accomplish her object softened the bitterness of disappointment. And although her husband does not take a place among the lights and benefactors of the world, to be honored in coming ages, the self-sacrifice and devotion of his faithful wife will help to keep alive his memory.

IV.

REVOLUTIONARY ECHOES.

The American Revolution—the sequence of events
through which thirteen insulated colonies severed
connection with the government that had founded
them, and established a federation of united states
—can never lose its interest for the American people.
Rather as time goes on and the marvelous outcome
of that severance and affiliation is more clearly manifested, there is increasing interest in searching out
and treasuring up every fact and incident connected
with this momentous revolution. Leaving primal
causes and underlying principles to be discussed by
the philosophic historian, our special object of inquiry is—What part did our own ancestors, the residents of these Windham County towns, bear in this
great struggle?

Our county of Windham, it may be noted, bore a
more prominent part in the revolutionary conflict
than her present position in Connecticut would indi-
cate. Her settlers were mainly of old Massachusetts
stock, closely connected by family ties with towns in
the vicinity of Boston. The main routes of travel from
Boston to Hartford and New York, Norwich and New

London; from Providence to Springfield and Norwich, ran through Windham County, bringing it into daily communication with business and political centres. The peculiar structure of the Connecticut town, its liberty to order and carry forward its own internal affairs, had developed in its inhabitants a spirit of inquiry and self-reliance. The money question was one that appealed with great force to these Windham County farmers. Obliged to tax themselves for the support of minister and schoolmaster, as well as for town and military expenses, every item of expenditure was most carefully scrutinized. The connection between taxation and representation had been early instilled into their minds. No town presumed to send representatives to legislature till it was able to pay its proportion of public charges. Its request for the privilege of sending deputies was always accompanied by lists of estates for assessments. Ministers exempt by law from tax-paying were not expected to vote. When, therefore, Great Britain's change of policy was indicated, when her claim to the right of enforcing direct tribute from every part of her dominions was made known, it roused immediate and intelligent opposition. The colonies rose as one in resistance to the Stamp Act. Prominent citizens of Windham County, Lawyer Dyer, Putnam, and Durkee, encouraged and abetted acts of open resistance. The liberties of the colonists were in jeopardy. When in the face of earnest remonstrance parliament persisted in its arbitrary course, imposing in 1767 taxes upon glass, paper, tea and other articles, they were met by determined and organized opposition. The committee appointed at a public meeting in Boston, October, 1767, prepared and sent out an explicit "form" in which the signers pledged themselves to encourage the use of American productions, and refrain from purchasing articles of European manufacture. In response to this call a most enthusiastic meeting was held at Windham Green, which resulted in the adoption of the following votes and measures, viz.:

"That we do engage with and promise each other that we will not from and after the first day of March next, by land or water, transport into this Colony either for sale or our own family's use, nor purchase of any other person, any of the following articles produced or manufactured out of North America, viz. : Loaf-sugar, cordage, coaches, chaises, and all sorts of carriages and harnesses for the same, men's and women's saddles, and bridles and whips, all sorts of men's hats, men's and women's apparel ready-made, men's gloves, women's hats, men's and women's shoes, sole-leather, shoe and knee buckles, iron ware, clocks, nails, gold, silver and thread lace, gold and silver buttons, diamond stone and paste ware, snuff, tobacco, mustard, clocks and watches, silversmith and jeweller's ware, broad-cloth that costs above 9s. pr. yard, muffs, tippets and all sorts of headdress for women, women's and children's stays, starch, silk and cotton velvet, linseed oil, lawn and cambric that costs above 4s. pr.

8*

yard, malt liquors, cheese, chairs and tables, and all kinds of
cabinet ware, horse combs, linen exceeding 2s. per yard, silks of
any kind in garments, men's and women's stockings, and wove
patterns for breeches and vests."

They also agreed to discourage and discountenance the excessive use of all foreign teas, spices,
and black pepper; also expensive treats by military
officers, and to encourage various specified domestic
manufactures, and to discountenance in the most effectual but decent and lawful manner any inhabitant
who did not conform to these regulations. They also
voted that a committee be appointed to correspond
with committees from the several towns in the
county, in order to render the foregoing proposals
as extensive and effectual as may be. This report
was unanimously adopted at " a very full meeting of
the inhabitants of the town," and three of her most
influential citizens—Nathaniel Wales, Jun., Samuel
Grey and Dr. Joshua Elderkin—appointed a committee of correspondence. The several towns of the
county were quick to follow this suggestion; held
indignation meetings; passed resolutions and appointed their best men on these corresponding committees.   According to Bancroft, Samuel Adams
"thought out his plan of correspondence and union
among the friends of Liberty," and laid it before a
Boston town meeting in 1772. Madam Mercy Warren claims that it had been previously discussed in

their home circle, and that her husband, Paymaster General James Warren, had suggested it to private friends. Like many other great movements it was "in the air," and Samuel Adams undoubtedly has the honor of its public and general enforcement. But here we have it in full force among our Windham County towns in December, 1767; five years in advance of its general adoption.

And these resolutions and pledges were not suffered to remain dead letters. If any of our young people could have had the good fortune to attend the wedding of Miss Dora Flint, of Windham Green, December, 1767, they must have discarded from their apparel every article of foreign manufacture. Silk, ribbons, gauze, lace, jewels, are rigidly tabooed. The wedding garment that wins admittance to that marriage feast is of sober homespun. The bountiful refreshments are all of native origin. Does not Connecticut furnish fish, fowl, and game in endless variety and abundance? Sparkling beverages are distilled from her own grapes and apples. Even the domestic red-root tea can be made wholesome and palatable. It was a jovial and joyful feast, attended by belles and beaux from Lebanon and Norwich, as well as Windham. Patriotic zeal flavored the viands and added lustre to the homespun, home-made garments. Any evasion or infringement of this agreement was quickly noted and held up to severest

reprobation. Joshua Elderkin, a prominent merchant, presuming to have on sale "felt hats and
worsted patterns," the town voted "To look upon
him as a person not fit to sustain any office of trust
till he properly manifests his repentance."

The tea question also came to the front in Windham. Perhaps there was no article whose deprivation
caused so much inconvenience and grumbling, and
none that seemed so obnoxious to flaming patriots.
"Any person who persists in using *tea* shows disregard for the liberties of America," votes the town of
Canterbury. The old minister in Scotland Parish had
the misfortune to lose his step-daughter, Elisabeth
Devotion, a beautiful young woman. Her illness was
sudden and severe; her death greatly afflictive; and
under the circumstances the aged parents were persuaded to indulge in the gentle stimulant of a cup of
tea. And such a storm as was raised by it. As soon
as Mr. Cogswell heard of the complaints he hastened
to the Committee of Inspection with certificates from
attendant physicians that the tea had been taken by
their advice as a medical prescription. But this excuse was wholly unsatisfactory. From all parts of
the parish parishioners were dropping into the minister's house to vent their own disapproval, and report
sayings of their neighbors. Some showed their dis-
pleasure by actually staying away from meeting.
Others insisted that Mr. Cogswell's dereliction should

be published and denounced in the Norwich and New London newspapers. One old woman declared that she should never be satisfied till Mr. Cogswell made public explanation and confession in the pulpit.

In the same town a good farmer had worked up a little barter trade with Newport. Some one surmising that *tea* might be among the articles brought home, neighbors met him on the road with a supply of tar and feathers ready for application had the obnoxious article been found in his saddle-bags.

Windham County's intimate relations with Boston and Providence brought her into touch with current events. A son of Pomfret—Darius Sessions—was deputy governor of Rhode Island at the time of the burning of the Gaspee. Woodstock boys assisted in throwing the tea into Boston harbor. Joseph Howe, pastor of New South Church, could give thrilling reports of the desolation wrought by the enforcement of the Boston Port Bill. That act of power had great effect in hastening the inevitable conflict. A day of public fasting and prayer was observed throughout Connecticut. On the day the bill took effect, June 1, 1774, meetings were held in most of the towns. In Lebanon, the home of Gov. Trumbull, the bells were tolled throughout the day; town house and public buildings draped with black. The people were everywhere aflame with indignation. Corresponding committees received new powers and in-

structions. Sympathetic words for the suffering
inhabitants of Boston were followed by helpful gifts.
Windham town was first in relief with her "small
flock" of two hundred and fifty-eight sheep. Putnam himself took down Brooklyn's gift of one hundred and twenty-five fine sheep. Plainfield, Pomfret,
Killingly, Woodstock, sent on their flocks. "A beef
cow for the distressed," with quaint words of sympathy was forwarded by Capt. Aaron Cleveland, of
Canterbury, father of the future Gen. Moses Cleveland.

As it became more and more evident that Great
Britain was bent upon carrying out her scheme of
taxation, the colonists became more earnest and determined in plans for resistance. "Millions for defence but not a cent for *tribute*," was the prevailing
sentiment. The burning words of Patrick Henry
and James Otis added fuel to flames. Military preparation was carried on by every possible means.
Experience gained in helping Great Britain to expel
the French from Canada was now turned to account
in training men to resist the authority of Great Britain. Connecticut equipped four new regiments in
the autumn of 1774. Each town was ordered to provide double its usual stock of powder, balls, and
flint. Trainings twice a month were required of
each military company. The militia organization of
our colony was then very efficient; military spirit,

high. Great military parades aroused the admiration and martial spirit of country lads. A brigade training in Plainfield, 1773, is especially memorable for inciting the first spark of military enthusiasm in a young Quaker from Rhode Island, Nathaniel Greene, destined to win a high name among revolutionary commanders. Equally noteworthy was a military gathering at Woodstock Hill, May, 1774—one of the first of Woodstock's "notable meetings." Soldiers in Indian dress caught up and carried away some of the children present but were pursued and brought back in triumph by Capt. McClellan's gallant "troop of horse," to the intense admiration of thousands of spectators.

But while providing guns, bullets, and powder, and exciting public spirit by loud harangues and spectacular exhibitions, they did not forget to fortify themselves with arguments. The most influential ministers of Windham County came out boldly in defence of the rights of the people. Rev. Ebenezer Devotion, of Scotland, was sent as Windham's representative during the Stamp Act agitation. A clause in the resolutions of the General Assembly, after passage of the Boston Port Bill, expresses the true Connecticut attitude of solid men at that epoch :

"That the subjects of his Majesty in this Colony ever have had and of right ought to have and enjoy all the liberties, immunities and privileges of free and natural-born subjects within

any of the dominions of our said King . . . as fully and
amply as if they and everyone of them were born within the
realm of England."

A small book widely circulated in Connecticut during this winter of 1774-75, and especially endorsed
by Windham County clergy, enforced this principle
in most effective terms. It was entitled—"English
Liberties, or the Freeborn subjects Inheritance, con-
taining Magna Charta, Habeas Corpus Act, a Declaration of the Liberties of the Subject, the Petition
of Right, and other kindred documents," reprinted
from the fifth English edition, and showing, saith the
preface, "the laws and rights that from age to age
have been delivered down to us from our renowned
forefathers, and which they so dearly bought and
vindicated to themselves at the expense of so much
blood and treasure." And yet there are those to-day
who ask if our country people were not "*dragooned*"
into rebellion by partisan leaders!

Fully to appreciate the part borne by Windham
County in the seven years' contest, we must bear in
mind the meagreness of her resources as compared
with the present. The population of the towns now
embraced in the county was a little over seventeen
thousand: its grand list of estates only figured at
about £160,000, considerably less than three-quarter
million dollars. There was no business centre of any
pretensions except at Windham Green, and the pop-

ulation of old Windham town, including village, Scotland, and parts of present Hampton and Chaplin territory, was only thirty-five hundred. Killingly, including all Thompson and present Putnam east of the Quinebaug, had about the same population as Windham, and its tax list only rated a little more than a hundred thousand dollars. A few houses in each town clustered about the hill meeting-house, but the main bulk of the population was scattered about in farm houses. There were a few stores in Windham: Larned and Mason carried on an extensive barter trade in Thompson Parish; there were saw and grist mills in every town, but the great majority of the inhabitants were farmers. Wonderment has been expressed at the large number of men kept in service during the war in proportion to the population. It was due mainly to the fact that the men were available; not tied up by business cares. These stalwart farmers with their large families of boys were more at liberty to answer the call than any succeeding generation.

The section was favored in the way of public roads. A weekly stage-coach from Providence to Norwich passed through Plainfield; a new route was established in 1774 from Norwich to Boston, passing through Windham, Pomfret, and Thompson. The only post-office was in New London. Taverns were numerous on every road, and well supplied with

9

liquor. Public life at this time mainly centered in
the town meeting and military gathering. Windham's military companies were comprised in the Fifth,
Eleventh, and Twenty-first Connecticut regiments—
strong and well disciplined organizations. Jedidiah
Elderkin was colonel, Experience Storrs, lieut.-colo-
nel of the Fifth, which comprised companies from
Windham and Ashford. Pomfret, Woodstock and
Killingly men made up the Eleventh—Ebenezer Williams, colonel; William Danielson, lieut.-colonel. The
newly organized 21st took in Plainfield and Canterbury. A " troop of horse " connected with each regiment was extremely popular. Old French war vete-
rans connected with the several companies added
much to their spirit and efficiency.

The news of the battle of Lexington found these
men ready for the summons. Thousands of hearts
and homes were stirred by the announcement. An
official despatch sent from Worcester reached Daniel
Tyler, Jun., Brooklyn, 8 A. M. April 20, the morning
after the encounter; but earlier than that, as we
learn from private sources, a swift-footed messenger
speeding across the hills brought the great news to
Woodstock and Killingly. A small boy then sleeping in bed with his grandfather—Ephraim, son of Dr.
Manasseh Cutler—tells the story in later years :

" I well remember that the express with the news of the battle of Lexington came directly to my grandfather's house in the

night. He was in bed and I slept with him. He arose and fired
his gun three times, which was doubtless the agreed signal as it
was universally expected there would be a hostile attack from
the British. Before sunrise be with fifteen others had started
for the battlefield. He had the care of a quantity of powder
which was kept in the meeting house. He gave directions to
have half a pound delivered to each man as he called for it. The
house was thronged through the day with parties of ten or
twenty men who followed on towards Boston. I suppose that
from the age of sixteen to seventy all left except sickness or
some disability excused them. I remember that while the men
were all away the women were thrown into quite a panic by a
report which was started by some mischievous or evil-disposed
person, that 'Malbones niggers' were coming to pillage and
burn the place. Our house was filled with trembling, frightened
women and children. There was not a firearm or weapon in the
place and only a few aged men. I remember they prepared ket-
tles of heated water and the boys were stationed as sentinels to
give timely notice of their approach. My place was the top of
my grandfather's gambrel-roofed house. But we saw no negroes
nor indeed anybody else for the whole place seemed deserted."

On this memorable day men from six companies
marched from Killingly. Those from the mother
town were led by Major William Danielson and captains Ephraim Warren and Joseph and Daniel Cady.
The Thompson men were led by captains Joseph Elliott and John Green and Lieutenant Elwell. Many
of the older men, the fathers of the town, were in the
ranks. The honored list of 177 names embraces representatives of nearly every old family in the large

town. Woodstock sent four companies under captains
Daniel Lyon, Ephraim Manning, Nathaniel Marcy,
Benjamin Lyon, with her proportion of the "troop
of horse," and of Elwell's New Boston company.
All the other towns in the county were worthily represented. We all know the story of Putnam's reception of the news and how much he had contributed
towards inciting military spirit and advising efficient
organization. The field in which he left his young
son, Daniel, to unyoke the team left in the furrow is
one of the hallowed possessions of Windham County.
His hurried ride that April day to Cambridge is
linked with that of Paul Revere in popular regard.

Among the many thousand homes that day engrossed by the great news and hurried preparations,
the one I see most clearly is a low, square old house,
now standing in South Woodstock, left of the road
that turns to Roseland Park. There the famous
Windham County "troop of horse" gathered around
their leader, Capt. Samuel McClellan—a stalwart
body of men, the pride of eastern Connecticut—and
thence they started off in advance of regimental orders—thirty-six horsemen in battle array. And after
all were gone in the late April afternoon, the mistress of the household—Rachel Abbe of Windham—
brought out a small bunch of saplings, stripling elms
from her early home, and with her own hands planted
them in Woodstock soil. And there they stand on

the common before the house, three noble elms, true
trees of Liberty, forever testifying to the patriotic
devotion of a daughter—rather let us say of a *mother*
of the Revolution—one whose constant aid and sympathy encouraged and strengthened her husband and
many other sons of Windham County to bear a most
honorable and helpful part in the long struggle.

What would we not give for as clear a glimpse of
many Pomfret homes on that memorable Saturday
and Sunday. All day and night the clans were mar-
shaling in this town. No promiscuous scramble to
the front was allowed in Putnam's town. By his
advice the companies of the Fifth Regiment were
mustered to march in due military order to the scene
of action. And here they met in Pomfret Street and
Abington, hundreds of men ready for marching
orders. It is strange that tradition preserves no hint
of that most remarkable gathering. We are indebted
to the diary of Lieut.-Col. Storrs for brief report.
Late on Saturday night he and his company reached
Pomfret and found Ashford and Windham companies
awaiting him. The officers were entertained at the
house of Mr. Ebenezer Grosvenor; the soldiers—
where? Did they bivouac in tents, or were they
billeted upon scores of Pomfret homes? Hundreds
more came in the night, eager to offer themselves for
service. As soon as possible after the morning meal
they sent for Rev. Mr. Putnam, the Pomfret minister,

9*

to pray with the companies. After prayer Col. Storrs
formed a hollow square and communicated regimental
orders. The men were then dismissed till 1 P. M.,
while the officers held council. Was service held
that day in that famous great meeting-house, filled
with those waiting soldiers? Did those good
ministers, Reverends Putnam and Ripley, improve
the opportunity for timely prayer and exhortation?
Did anxious wives and mothers leave household cares
to attend these helpful services? No echo comes to
us from those waiting, eager men and burdened
households. We can only picture in our minds the
bustle, the excitement, the varied experiences of that
eventful day in many a Pomfret home. Col. Storrs
curtly notes that they decided to take one *fifth* of the
ten companies present and order the "overplush" to
return home. The elect two hundred were from Ashford and Windham, (Canada Parish) with fifty-nine
from Pomfret. At 5 P. M. they started on their
march to Lexington. Lieut.-Col. Storrs accompanied
them as far as Dudley and then left them in charge
of Capt. Thomas Knowlton—a young hero already
noted in military service, and destined to win immortal laurels. These companies were received with
much distinction at Cambridge, as the first on the
ground fully disciplined and equipped. Other Pomfret men—Lieut. Keyes, Corporal Seth Grosvenor,
Dr. Waldo, and a number of privates, had preceded
with the Troop.

Of these thousands of Windham County men who sallied out upon the alarm, the younger portion almost without exception served under successive enlistments during the war. As many as were needed were mustered into Putnam's own regiment—the Connecticut Third, in May. The captains of its ten companies were Israel Putnam, senior and junior, Experience Storrs, John Durkee, Obadiah Johnson, Thomas Knowlton, James Clark, Ephraim Manning, Joseph Elliott, Ebenezer Mosely. The older men were left to carry on their farms and town affairs, but were often called out with the militia.

We catch few inside glimpses of affairs this summer of 1775—the busiest and happiest summer of the war for New England. As yet all were in the first flush of novelty and excitement. Every patriot home was astir with eager preparation. Constant intercourse was maintained with the camp at Cambridge. Many an aged Jesse "went down to camp" or sent his fresh young David as a substitute. The report of the battle at Bunker Hill thrilled every patriot heart. Windham County bore a most honorable part in this memorable battle. Putnam, by general acclamation, was made the hero of the day. Knowlton and Grosvenor had done conspicuous service. Companies from Windham, Ashford, Canterbury, and Pomfret had taken part in the main defence. Others from Killingly had helped cover the retreat when

ammunition was exhausted.   The names of eleven
Windham County men left on the field are inscribed
on the sacred roll of Bunker Hill monument.

A mother's letter brings us back into the home circle.   It is from Mrs. Samuel Gray, of Windham, to
her son, Lieut. Ebenezer Gray.

" JULY 81, A, D. 1775.

Dear Child :—I, this morning heard by Mr. Trumbull, who
passed through town in haste last evening, that you are preparing to meet the enemy, or to drive them from their new intrench-
ments.   I could not hear it without some emotion of soul, although I firmly believe God is able to deliver and will deliver
us out of the hands of these unnatural enemies in his own time.
Our cause is just I don't doubt, and God in his holy and righteous providence has called you there to defend our just rights
and privileges.   I would commit you into the hands of a just
and merciful God, who alone is able to defend you.   Confessing
my utter unworthiness of the least mercy, would trust in un-
merited mercy through Jesus Christ for all that strength, courage and fortitude that you stand in need of in the business he is
calling you to.   Trust in the Lord and be of good courage ; the
eye of the Lord is upon them that fear him ; upon them that
hope in his mercy.   Confess your sins daily before the Lord,
and forsake every evil way ; walk in all the commandments of
the Lord.   Be careful to set a good example before those that are
under you, especially in observing the Sabbath.   The surest way
of conquering our enemies is to turn from every evil way, and
seek the Lord with all our hearts with confession of our sins.   I
am more afraid of our sins than of all the forces of our enemy.
As to profane swearing, which is very common in camps, I al-

ways thought you were not inclined to, and I trust you will take all possible care to prevent it in those that fall under your care.

I think we have abundant reason to praise the name of the Lord for his wonderful assistance and deliverances our people have experienced at one time and another, especially at Bunker's Hill. Well, may we say, ' Had it not been the Lord who was on our side when such a number of troops rose up and surrounded our people, then they had swallowed us up quick when their wrath was kindled against us.' These merciful assurances of God for us ought to encourage us to call upon God, and strengthen our faith in Him. That you may put your trust in God, and go on with courage and fortitude to whatever work or business you may be called to, is the sincere prayer of your Loving Mother.

LYDIA GRAY."

And some homes, even in this first hopeful summer, are already darkened. A neat farm-house on the road to Grosvenordale—the residence of our late friend, Mr. Elliott Shumway—brings freshly before me our first Revolutionary officer, Capt. Joseph Elliott, tossing on his bed through the hot summer days. A brave and gallant officer in the prime of life, after return from Lexington he had been selected to lead the Killingly company of Putnam's own regiment. There is reason for belief that he, with part of his company, covered the retreat of the little band from the redoubt at Bunker Hill, preserving it from annihilation or capture. A few days later he is at home struggling with disease, doubtless brought on by fatigue and exposure. We picture him lying in

the darkened house, and the bereaved wife, the eight
children, and aged grandfather following him to his
grave in early August.

And the minister's house on Killingly Hill lies in
deep shadow. There in June had been welcomed a
son of the house, Rev. Joseph Howe, the beloved
pastor of New South Church, Boston—driven from
his pulpit by the exigencies of the time—the most
brilliant young man of his generation. Passing on
to visit friends in Hartford, he succumbed suddenly
to complicated disease, brought on by fatigue and
excitement. The death of his step-father, Rev.
Aaron Brown, while returning from his funeral, made
the blow still heavier for family and people.

Even a deeper shadow rested on a stately residence
at Windham Green, the home of Col. Eleazer Fitch,
high sheriff of the county. That beautiful home, so
famed for social attraction and musical culture, was
now closed and barred by outside pressure. A colonel
in the old French war—a civil officer under the King
—Col. Fitch could not take sides with the patriots
in resistance to royal authority. His words of reprobation roused the ire of the inflammable people of
Windham. A boycott was served upon him. A paper
was circulated in which the signers pledged themselves to withhold from Col. Fitch every possible accommodation. A miller must not grind; a blacksmith must not renew a horseshoe for a Tory—and

this loyal gentleman who had been the idol of his
generation, "the best looking man in the army,"
lived in isolation and loneliness, lacking the common
comforts of life—"Bad weather for Tories," reports
Col. Storrs, "yet we have some."

To a certain extent it is easy to follow the course
of events during the Revolutionary period. We
have official military records, details of public meetings, outline reports of movements and engagements
in the limited newspaper of the day, but we know
that much occurred of which we can gain no knowledge. It is a matter of wonderment that of home
life we have so few glimpses, and yet we know that
every home in the colonies was most intimately
affected. Even where father, husband or son was
not in actual service there was depreciation of currency, diminution of supplies, interruption of the
common routine of life. Public and private life, in
town and home, were alike pivoted upon the war that
was in progress.

Personally I have to confess great mis-improve-
ment of privileges. My maternal grandmother was
eighteen years of age at the close of the war, and afterwards married a revolutionary soldier, yet all that
I gained from her was a chance allusion that impressed my youthful sensibilities of "bloody tracks
left by the soldiers in marching." "I was born,"
says our good old minister, Daniel Dow, "in 1772,

and have a vivid recollection of many of the important events of the Revolutionary War "—and yet,
though Doctor and Mrs. Dow were capital story tel-
lers, ever ready to communicate, not one of those
" vivid recollections " has been preserved by parish-
ioner or descendant. I think I have seen but one
revolutionary soldier, " Old Sibley "—who lived near
the village. The boys of my time thought it great
fun to hear his war stories, but the girls did not go
for him. Pomfret Factory boys in the Quinebaug
valley had the rare privilege of hearing live Bunker
Hill stories from that worthy officer of the church
militant—Dea. Elihu Sabin. He would tell them of
his covering the retreat from the Hill and being confronted by a fierce-looking British officer when he
had but one charge left in his musket.

" And did you kill him ? " the boys would ask
eagerly.

" Wall," he would answer deliberately, " I dunno
exactly, but the last I see of him he was getting off
his horse."

It is because of the increasing rarity of such first-
hand incidents that we should take much pains to
avail ourselves of every possible source of information ; to gather and note down every fact and item
received from those who were personally connected
with the Revolution. The time is not far distant
when the last person will have passed away who has
even *seen* a Revolutionary soldier.

With the transfer of the seat of war from Boston
to New York, came far heavier burdens to our Windham County towns. No more pleasant intercourse
with the camp; no more return of sick and wounded
to be nursed at home. But far more urgent was the
demand and larger the number of those now entering upon service. All the provision that could be
spared from household supplies was brought forward
for the use of the army. Every grain of salt, every
scrap of saltpetre was carefully hoarded. Housewives ransacked their stores for towcloth for tent and
knapsack. One-fourth of the men in each militia
regiment, perfectly equipped with arms, balls, flints,
and other needful articles, were ordered to hold
themselves ready to march as minute-men at the
shortest notice; while recruiting for the several new
regiments ordered by Government was pushed forward with greatest activity. A letter from Washington, June 29, to Brig.-Gen. Wadsworth, hastens preparations—"The safety of our army under Heaven
depends upon the seasonable arrival of the Connecticut regiments at New York." Woodstock companies were ordered to set out, Thursday, July 4. If
the whole company was not in readiness they were
to start with twenty-five men, forwarding the remainder as fast as they became ready " with all convenient speed." Do we wonder that such a summons
sent a thrill through every soldier's home? How

10

great the danger they were facing in that strange
far-off New York and Jersey! Yet they went by
twos and threes from many a Woodstock home.
Two sons went out from Henry Child's tavern—one
son, at least, from the home of that leading patriot,
Capt. Elisha Child, and a young man brought up in
the family. While all were engrossed with final
preparations and words of cheer and counsel, this
orphan youth, thinking that should he fall in the
campaign there were none to remember or mourn for
him, stole off in the woods for a memorial tree which
he set out in front of this old Ephraim Child house—
and thus East Woodstock gained her "Revolutionary
elm "—a grand old tree, as strong and thrifty as the
nation it typifies. Little did those Woodstock men
realize, as they marched off for service that morning
of July 4, 1776, the significance of the events in
which they were participating. Days passed before
they even heard of that memorable Declaration that
hallows that day forever to every son and daughter
of our land. But we may well believe that its spirit
was in their hearts, and in the hearts of their townsmen, who, though they had already sent out " a much
greater number than their proportion," now pledged
themselves anew " to do everything in their power to
advantage the public cause." A letter from Washington's own hand, commending them for their self-
sacrifice in sparing their beloved minister, Rev. Abiel

Leonard, to serve continuously as chaplain in Putnam's regiment, was an additional stimulus. And Mr. Leonard's example and eloquent exhortations doubtless had great influence. As an instance of the sympathetic enthusiasm of the women, it is said that when in the preceding autumn some soldiers returned home when their term of enlistment had expired without waiting for formal discharge, that their wives gave them a hearty scolding and threatened to drive them back to the camp.

And now this courage and enthusiasm were to be sorely tested. This campaign of 1776 in Long Island and New York, brought a severe strain upon Connecticut. She furnished by far the largest number for the field; her losses were very heavy. The battle and retreat from Long Island, the hurried stampede through New York city, the death of Knowlton, the sickness raging in the camp—all brought inexpressible distress to the homes of these Windham County soldiers. The regular quota of men from the several towns were mustered into Colonels Ward and Durkee's regiments for the year's service. Another call was made in June for special service in Wadsworth's Brigade, at Long Island and New York city. A still more urgent call in September summoned the Eleventh Regiment, militia, with all speed to New York. A hundred and twelve men now went out from Killingly, and equal proportion from other towns, in-

cluding every man that was fit for service. These
were indeed "the times that tried men's souls" in
camp and home. Every post brought tidings of fresh
loss and disaster. The few letters that reached home
told of defeat, sickness, suffering, imprisonment, and
death. Here is a letter from Private Thomas Dike,
who went out from Thompson Parish in the Eleventh
Regiment :

" WESTCHESTER, Sept. ye 10th, 1776.

Ever Honored Father and Mother :

After my duty to you hoping these few lines will find you all
well as through the goodness of God it leaves me at present, I
would inform you that I arrived here last night and have made
all the inquiries after Samuel that I have had opportunity for but
cannot hear where he is. The last account was that last Saturday
he was sick and in the hospital in the city of New York and
came that day from the hospital up to the regiment but being
weak could not travel and several of the company told me there
were carriages provided to carry the sick over to the Jersey side
among which was Sergeant Jesse Larned who is since dead,
Samuel Dike, Amos Green and many others. I hope to hear soon
from him, and see him for they tell me he is much discouraged
but thought he was getting better.

There has been a sore battle at York. The Regulars landed
on the island of York, both on the North and East Rivers on
Sabbath day, and our men were obliged to retreat with all possible speed, but notwithstanding many were killed and taken.
Capt. Stephen Crosby being over hot went into a house and
drinked cold water and died immediately. Lieut. Buck is either
killed or taken prisoner and several more Killingly men. On
Monday it is reported our men got the better ; killed and took

great numbers of the Regulars and Hessians. Col. Williams' regiment is ordered off to the Jersey side and we expect to go from here to-day. It is very sickly here among the militia. William Smith and Ebenezer Nichols we left behind. Solomon Smith and John Barrett must stop here or return back. The Lord be merciful to us all for we have got where the inhabitants show no pity. I beg your prayers for me that I may be preserved from sin, sickness and the sword and be soon returned to my family and friends whom I am greatly concerned for. I would have written a few lines to my wife but have not time. Now, I hope she will not take it hard. I desire to be remembered to her and all my friends. Tell my little children I long to see them but when I shall I cannot tell. It is all confusion here.

Your dutiful son,   THOMAS DIKE."

Still more distressing pictures were given by Oliver Grosvenor, Commissary of Eleventh Regiment, in letters to his wife:

" The sick daily increases in numbers : some companies not more than two or three in their returns fit for duty : the rest sick and taking care of the sick. . . . It is not in my power to paint you the doleful scenes I behold every hour : neither did I believe that rational creatures could be divested of that humanity that I find they are subject to in the camps, where sickness and sin so much prevail. Alas for our land which now mourns beneath the horrors and distresses of our present war. . . . Six of our regiment have died since the day before yesterday and now there are a number I expect to hear are dead in the morning. OCT. 8, 1776."

The irregularity of communication enhanced distress and anxiety. In the longer or shorter interval

10*

between these chance letters imagination painted
even greater losses and horrors. Yet the true reality
was beyond expression. Scores of men who had gone
out full of life and spirits, blotted out of sight never
to be seen again by friend or kindred. Some were in
the flush of youth and hope. Some left young brides;
others the burdened wife with family of little children.
It is well perhaps that we cannot look in upon these
bereaved homes. Knowlton's, with its eight children;
Capt. Crosby's with six, and in both instances a child
born after the decease of its father. This captain of
ours was, like Capt. Elliott, a man of sterling character, who had represented the town at the General
Court in 1775. His little son Stephen, not four years
old, remembered through life his opening the gate
for his father as he rode out for the last time, and his
"God bless you, my son," as he stooped from his
saddle. And there were many more equally dear and
precious buried where they fell in New York and
Jersey. No sending home of loved remains.

> " 'Tis little, but it looks in truth
>   As if the quiet bones were blest
>   Amid familiar scenes to rest,
>   And in the places of its youth."

But even this small consolation was denied the
Revolutionary soldier, and even in many cases a stone
to mark his burial place. Even when he died at

home the memorial stone was withheld or long delayed. The poverty of the times is shown by this
omission. The widow with her little ones, the aged
parents deprived of their strong sons, could not afford
the cost. But their memory was tenderly cherished,
and years after their decease their names were inscribed on the stones in the old burying ground that
marked the graves of wife or parent. It is remarkable to find so many of these delayed inscriptions in
our own Thompson ground. The names of Captains
Elliott and Crosby appear on the grave-stones with
their widows, who had survived them nearly forty
years. The names of two and even three sons dying
in New York and New Jersey are carved below those
of aged parents. But the resting place of those who
died in camp or fell in battle was seldom known to
their friends.

Those were indeed dark days alike in Jersey camp
and Windham County farm-house. The soldier in
camp and hospital was burdened with anxieties for
those at home. Heavy, indeed, were the cares of
those wives and mothers. Young lads were called
upon to bear the brunt of autumn work and household provision. One little lad in Thompson, only six
years old, remembered vividly through life his trials
in going after the cows those November twilights, his
bare feet entangling in the briars, his little summer
suit of towcloth so tattered that he could hardly

hold it together as he stumbled about the rocky pasture.

But the darkest day has gleams of light. Amid the anxieties and distress of this terrible autumn came the most ludicrous episode of the war; a farce between the acts of a sombre tragedy. Yet, to the actors it was a most real experience and illustrates one of the most trying features of the situation—isolation from the seat of war and difficulty of obtaining accurate information. It occurred in the vicinity of the Great Elm, in what was called the "South Neighborhood" of Thompson Parish, after the last call for militia. The army had been driven from New York; British fleets were in the Sound threatening New London and Providence; affairs were in the greatest confusion and rumors flew thick from every quarter. New London and Providence were burned; Connecticut was invaded; the victorious British might be expected to sweep through the State at any moment. Besides these general dangers this section was haunted by a special bugbear.

Right down in Brooklyn the Tory and churchman, Malbone, owned a gang of negro slaves, and just north of Thompson there was a remnant of " Paygan Injins " occupying a reservation. Combustible material was kept piled up on conspicuous hills for signal warning in case of attack, and a kettle of tar was suspended from the cross-bar of the Liberty pole on

Killingly Hill, for the same purpose. A single spark of rumor lighted all these combustibles. A post galloped through town without stopping to communicate news, and a saucy boy on Dudley Hill had his ears boxed by a suspected Tory. Quick through the town flew the report of immediate onset.

"The Tor-ies are coming! The Tor-ies are coming," was the awe-struck cry, and when it reached the elm tree the tale was magnified by the addition of "Malbone Niggers" and "Paygan Injins" burning and slaughtering everything before them. What a terrible prospect! There was not an able-bodied man in the corner. Nothing but women and children, old-folks and invalids. Panic, dire, unreasoning, frenzied panic took possession. All manner of ridiculous things were said and done. Concealment and flight seemed the only course of action. And so the neighbors, old and young, rushed together and started off pell-mell for a bushy swamp. One woman staid behind—the heroine of the day. I am always glad to relate the prowess of my much respected grandmother—Rebekah (Wilkinson) Larned —a worthy daughter of Liberty and Rhode Island. She was not the woman to desert her husband's property, or quail before Malbone and his negroes. Three young children and her husband's aged grandmother were in her care. Piling wood upon the ample fireplace, every iron implement that could be mustered

was thrust into the blazing coals, and from every
hook on the crane a kettle of water was suspended,
and had the foe appeared he would have met a hot
reception from fire and tongue. In vain did the fugitives send beseeching pleas. "Tell Becky," they
whimpered, " hot irons will never do for the British."
In vain did they urge the aged grandmother—the
widow of Justice Joseph Leavens—to share their
flight. Her faith surpassed her fears, and sinking
back into her chimney corner she meekly murmured
—" If I *am* to be killed by the Tor-ies to-night why
then I *shall be*, so I'll een stay with Becky."

But Tory and negro alike failed to materialize.
The great alarm proved a mere fizzle, but coming as
it did on those anxious days, it served a most admirable purpose. All the ridiculous sayings and doings
of the terrified were remembered and reproduced
with the vividness of instantaneous photograph. We
see Sam. Cheese ramming down bullets into his musket without any powder ; and poor, old, palsied Capt.
Merriam, with pitchfork quivering in his hands, as he
tried to guard and hold the house door. We catch
the sly gleam in the eye of the bedridden granny,
forgotten and left behind in the flurry, who had managed to crawl out of bed and stow herself away in a
cupboard. We hear the plaintive voice of poor old
hobbling Uncle Asa on his way to the swamp—
"Thithter, thithter, I've forgot my thin plathter,"

and the sister's brusque rejoinder, " Come along, Asa,
you'll *never* dress your shins again in this world,"
while Aunt Nabby voiced the general desire in her
heartfelt ejaculation—"I'd give a wedge of goold as
big as my foot for *one good dram*." It is truly re-
freshing to learn that these much tried sufferers had
so legitimate a cause for merriment, even if it is a
little hard on the panic-stricken subjects.

Probably the scarcity of Tories in Windham County
invested them with abnormal terror. In other parts
of the State they were sufficiently obvious, but here
they were too few to assert themselves. Poor Col.
Fitch, now deprived of his official position, sat solitary in his suspected mansion, barely supplied with
the every day necessities of life. Dr. Walton, of
Killingly, a bitter Tory, who once presumed to hide
a wounded British officer in his house, dared not open
his mouth. Hannah Miller, fleeing from Boston " as
from a nest of hornets to the happy and peaceful
town of Pomfret," with a hogshead of rum and tierce
of coffee for subsistence, was obliged to give proof
of her loyalty to the patriot cause before she could
settle down to the consumption of her rum and coffee.
Col. Malbone, chevalier and churchman, with his
" church parson and gang of negro slaves," felt constrained to observe extreme quiet, and restrict church
service and prayers for the king to his private residence. The saddest home in Windham County was

that of Nathan Frink, Pomfret's dashing young
lawyer and excise officer, who, after attempting to act
with the patriots, turned squarely against them and
entered the British army. His aged parents went
down unto the grave mourning, and a large circle of
relatives was overwhelmed with grief and mortifica-
tion. The August of 1777 brought grief to many
hearts in the death of Woodstock's beloved pastor,
Rev. Abiel Leonard, D. D. Mr. Leonard had won
much favor among his own people and the churches
of the county before his acceptance of the chaplaincy
of Putnam's regiment. Here he achieved still greater
popularity, his eloquent and patriotic discourses exciting much admiration. He may be said to have
been the father of "Army Literature"—"a prayer
composed for the benefit of the soldiers in the American army to assist them in their private devotions,"
and printed in a tract of nine pages, is noted as the
first attempt in this line. Washington's letter to the
Woodstock church may well be forever associated
with the memory of this honored pastor, viz.:

" *To the Church and Congregation at Woodstock :*

Mr. Leonard is a man whose exemplary life and conversation
must make him highly esteemed by every person who has the
pleasure of being acquainted with him. It therefore can be no
surprise to us to hear they are loth to part with him His influence in the army is great. He is employed in the glorious
work of attending to the morals of a brave people who are fight-

ing for their liberties—the liberties of the people of Woodstock
—the liberty of all America. We therefore hope that, knowing
how nobly he is employed, the congregation of Woodstock will
cheerfully give up to the public a gentleman so very useful.
And when, by the blessing of a kind Providence, this glorious
and unparalleled struggle for our liberties is at an end, we have
not the least doubt but Mr. Leonard will, with redoubled joy,
be received in the open arms of a congregation so very dear to
him as the good people of Woodstock are.

This is what is hoped for—this is what is expected, by the
congregation of Woodstock's sincere well wishers and very
humble servants,

GEORGE WASHINGTON,

ISRAEL PUTNAM

Head Quarters, Cambridge, }
  24th of March, 1776."   }

Washington's kind hope for the happy return of
the beloved pastor to his flock at the close of the
war was not destined for fulfillment, and the circumstances attending his death left a cloud upon his
memory. Dying at Danbury, on his way home from
the army, from wounds received by his own hand,
the real facts were not ascertained by his friends.
The story as handed down in Woodstock, upon what
seemed creditable authority, represented him as having overstaid a furlough, on account of the serious illness of his child—and that on his way back to camp
he was met by the tidings that he had been censured
and dismissed from his position. Keenly sensitive
to public opinion he could not endure this disgrace,

11

and attempted suicide. A letter recently come to
light, from Dea. Jedidiah Morse—the honored father
of an illustrious house—gives the true facts and
complete vindication. It was addressed to President
Wheelock, Dartmouth College, immediately after the
tidings of his decease had reached them, 18 Aug.
1777. He gives " a short, exact, but very melancholy
account of the death of his dear minister;" of his
being "as much set by in the army by Gen. Washington and other officers " as any man in the service;
of having a present of three hundred dollars made
him by Congress for special services, and that after
receiving liberty from his people to continue in the
army he thought prudent to take the small-pox by
inoculation, which detained him sometime and left
him in a poor state of health. That he then returned
to the army in the Jerseys ; took a tour to Philadel-
phia, where he preached before Congress to their
great satisfaction ; met with the Presbytery and had
the honorary title of Doctor of Divinity conferred
upon him. But during this time he was observed
"to be melancholy and cast down, and mind and
senses greatly disordered." On this Sunday he attended public worship, and went to bed apparently
as well as usual, but an unusual noise in his chamber
aroused the people of the house and they found him
in his gore, his throat cut but not dead. He was
able in a few days to bear removal to Danbury, but

the heat of the weather and raging of his wound
were too much for him and he passed away August
14th.

Melancholia caused by nervous exhaustion undoubtedly led to this unhappy act so much misunder-
stood even by his own dear people. We have great
reason for gratitude to Dea. Morse for leaving us the
inmost details of this sad end to a brilliant career—
and clearing the character of a devoted and self-
sacrificing patriot. In this instance there was no
deliberate attempt to blacken character and depreci-
ate service as there has been with others. It is bad
enough to malign the living in the heat of political
controversy, but they have a chance to correct and
live down misrepresentation; but in cold blood to
pick to pieces and tear down the reputation of public
men who did their best in times of difficulty and
danger, is most dastardly and ungrateful. We do
not claim perfection for our dead heroes—the best
of men are only human. But even indiscriminate
hero-worship is better than hero-demolition. The
great men who have helped in any way to make our
country what it is are our best heritage, and we cannot afford to have them belittled or taken away from
us by this spirit of carping criticism.

We, as Windham County people, have great reason
to complain of the treatment our own Putnam has
received at the hands of rivals and critics. Perhaps

the most remarkable specimen in this line is the statement recently made by one of these self-appointed
critics in the *New York Sun :* "That Gen. Putnam has
neither lateral nor lineal descendant living, although
a few families claim without any foundation such descent." If other charges against our old hero are
equally baseless we can afford to let them slide.

The summer of 1778 brought many Windham
County homes into close connection with the front
through Sullivan's Rhode Island campaign. An attempt was made in concert with the newly-arrived
French fleet to drive the British army from Newport
and Rhode Island. Windham County was called upon
to furnish all the aid in her power—ammunition,
cartridges, provisions for man and beast, and above
all, with soldiers. A Windham County company was
stationed on this field for the year, and companies of
her militia served at different periods. My maternal
great-uncle, Theodore Gay, went out for his first
campaign, with one of these companies. Though
living in the vicinity of the Great Elm, my grandfather's family had not shared in that memorable
alarm. The good deacon and his three oldest sons
were indeed absent in service, but Joseph and Theodore, though only seventeen and fifteen years of age,
felt quite equal to the situation. But they did not
trust in carnal bullets, nor even in hot water and
irons. Going on with their usual day's work, they

then proceeded with the "nightly chores," and after
supper sat down in the big kitchen with grandmother,
mother, and sister, read comforting words from the
great family Bible, and offered the accustomed evening prayer. Two of the brothers died that autumn
in Jersey, and now the bright young Theodore, God's
latest, best gift to the household, was sacrificed to the
Rhode Island campaign. A terrible norther swept
down at the beginning of the action, drove the French
fleet far south, and rendered futile months of careful
preparation. Many of our soldiers died from the
effect of cold and exposure, never seen again by those
at home who had sent them out so cheerily.

Another calamity, greatly afflicting many Windham County homes that same discouraged 1778, was
the Indian massacre at Wyoming, Penn. Some of
the most enterprising and promising young men in a
number of towns had taken their families to this
beautiful valley, and were among the victims of Indian barbarity. Conflicting rumors brought to Connecticut homes were followed by weeks of anxious
suspense, and then by the arrival of hapless widows,
foot-sore and destitute, with orphan families of eight,
ten, and, in the case of Mrs. Esther Minor Yorke, of
Voluntown, twelve children.

But enough of loss and disaster. There is a
brighter side to the picture. There are gleams of
light behind the clouds. As years passed on and it

11*

became increasingly evident that the colonies could
not be brought under subjection to the British yoke,
hope revived in patriot hearts. If in some cases the
war wrought demoralization, in a far greater number it stimulated energy, courage, self-reliance, self-
sacrifice. With unfailing constancy our Windham
County towns kept up their quotas of soldiers and
supplies. Lads who had so faithfully helped their
mothers in home and farm, grew up to take their
father's place in camp and council. It was a time of
rapid quickening and development. How it brought
out the stamina of our women. We mourn over the
comparative inconspicuousness of the Pilgrim mothers; we feel they do not receive their just meed of
honor and remembrance. Few of the stately colonial dames are brought to actual knowledge. But
the Revolutionary period not only brings to personal
recognition Mary and Martha Washington, Abigail
Adams, Mercy Warren, Faith Trumbull, Lucretia
Shaw, and the honored names affixed to scores of
Chapters, but called out unsuspected energy and faculty in thousands of humbler homes. The soldier on
the field was sustained and carried forward to final
victory by the labor and sympathy of the woman in
the home. How bravely they bore the heavy burdens brought upon them. We see them caring for
their stock, carrying on their farms, making the hay,
gathering their own supply of fuel, manufacturing

cloth, preparing their own tea and molasses, besides attending to everyday domestic affairs and training their children. Women trained to use the pen were called to write the household letters for less favored sisters. Some special feats of workmanship are reported. Mrs. Elisha Adams, of Brooklyn, lays down her floor and finishes her apartment. The women of Hampton, assisted by a lame old carpenter, raised the frame and assisted in building a large two-story house that has stood the wear of over a century. It was in this same vicinity that a suit of clothes was evolved from a sheep's back in less than two days.

The son came home in rags, and the sheep was sheared and bundled away in the cellar, while its wool was spun, woven, and made up into a substantial suit of clothes in time for the young soldier to wear back to camp in triumph. Here, too, little Mary Stedman, the ten-year-old kinswoman of the poet, Edmund C. Stedman, wrought out with her own small fingers a web of tow-cloth, carding, spinning, and weaving, exchanging it at Windham Green for a set of silver tea-spoons, now held as priceless heirlooms by her descendants. Among the thousand private, beneficent acts called out by the exigencies of the time, I like to include that of an aged widow, in Thompson—Mrs. Elisabeth (Hosmer) Alton—who kept through the summer a barrel of freshly brewed

beer on tap by the doorstep for the especial refresh-
ment of any passing soldier.

A somewhat quixotic expedition gave me a glimpse
of two Revolutionary homes under rather peculiar
aspect. The friend who enticed me had the good fortune to grow up at the feet of a great-grandmother,
and was particularly impressed by her yearnings for
the scene of her early married life, in a remote corner of Woodstock, where she had reared and buried
children, and so a century later we started off to
visit this "old Bolles homestead." We had some
difficulty in finding anyone to direct us in our search,
but after we had fairly recovered the trail, and the
old house came in view, it was wonderful how the
old stories of her youth came back to my companion :

" O, there's the great house fronting south just as grandmother
described it, and there is the very same great stone doorstep
where she stood parleying with the officers who had come to
search for a deserter. He was a poor, little, young fellow from
the neighborhood and had fared so hard they all pitied him, and
so grandmother talked with the officers on the doorstep while he
slunk out of the pantry window. Why, don't you see in that
little projection at the end of the house there's the very window
and he ran down the hill to this same bridge we are crossing and
then up the hill on the other side, running backward through the
snow so as to muddle up the track to a house right over the hill.
Why, there's the roof and chimney of that very house, and he
went in there and flung himself down before old Goody Blake
who was spinning at her wheel and begged her to save him from

the officers in pursuit. Well she had had wild boys of her own
and knew how to feel for him, so she just raised a trap-door and
stowed him away under the floor, and spreading a rug over the
door set her spinning-wheel upon it and when the officers came
on there she was spinning away at her wheel and innocently
humming a psalm tune."

In these later years, as the armies moved southward, there was less immediate connection and personal communication with the seat of war. Our little Ephraim Cutler, who, sleeping in bed with his
grandfather, caught the first echo of " the shot heard
round the world," now enlightened the neighborhood
at Killingly Hill by reading aloud " The New London Gazette " every Sabbath noon. The house would
be filled with elderly people, mothers and grandfathers, anxious to hear the news. One of the most
harrowing days during the whole period was that
Thursday afternoon in 1781, when residents of the
south part of the county heard the roar of the can-
non and saw the flames of consuming New London.
Men hastened to the scene and saw with their own
eyes the terrible butchery and destruction, more
dreadful from the thought that one of their own favored sons had been most active in this outrage.

Aside from this terrible experience and other New
London and Rhode Island alarms, there was less distress and suffering during these closing years. For
one thing, supplies were more plentiful. Success in

privateering brought to New London West India goods and even articles of luxury. And these goods were so carried about through the country that a bridal outfit was no longer limited to homespun. One glimpse in this line we leave with you for a parting picture.

A young girl in Pomfret is musing upon the question of a wedding dress—a lovely young girl with a face of rare promise and character—among whose numerous descendants are Mrs. Louise Chandler Moulton and Mrs. Caroline Fairfield Corbin. She knows the difficulty of the times, the scantiness of money and the many demands upon the father's purse, but a suitable dress for this supreme occasion in a young girl's life she *must have*. A peddler comes along with heavy packs. No matter where he got his goods: they are wonderful—and among them is the most beautiful piece of dainty pink satin that ever gladdened the eyes of prospective bride. She glances at the gruff old father, puzzling with knotted brow over his accounts. She does not dare to ask the favor, but the satin must be hers. Gathering around her the glistening folds she steals across the room, and kneeling at her father's feet, looks up with pleading eyes. And the grim old father catches on. Without a word spoken on either side he unlocks his desk and puts in his daughter's hand *forty* silver dollars, and the dainty pink satin soon figures at the marriage feast as the bride's gown and the bridegroom's waistcoat. And so, after our many sombre pictures, we leave you with this gladsome tableau-vivant, typifying, we believe, the happy days that were in store for the young republic, when, after the long, weary struggle, came the blessing of assured peace and perfected Union.

> " Thou too sail on, O ship of State,
> Sail on O Union, strong and great . . .
> Our hearts, our hopes, our prayers, our tears,
> Our faith, triumphant o'er our fears,
> Are all with thee, are all with thee."

V.

WINDHAM COUNTY AND PROVIDENCE.

The capital of Rhode Island and this northeast
corner of Connecticut have held close and continuous
relations. And even before there was a Providence
or a Windham County, before a sectional boundary
line had crossed the face of New England territory
and its fields and forests lay open to wild beasts and
wilder savages, these sections held continuous communication. The Narragansetts claimed right to
territory east of the Quinebaug river. The great
lake — Chan-bon-a-gong-a-monk (bound-mark) now
in Webster—marked the bound between sea-board
Narragansetts and inland Nipmucks, dwelling in
Nipnet — the pond or fresh water country. The
stronger Narragansetts held in close subjection the
feeble clans or tribelets of Nipmucks. Tradition
preserved but one instance of successful revolt, interesting to us as showing the early date of that peculiar
Rhode Island institution—the original, aboriginal,
perennial *clambake*.

The Nipmuck tributaries in the vicinity of Lake
Mashapaug (now Alexander's) were invited to partake
of a shore dinner of shell-fish, which it need hardly

be said they devoured with great relish. But when
their hosts in due time returned the visit, nothing
was offered them but lamprey eels served without
dressing. The daintier Narragansetts scoffed at this
plain fare and a free fight followed, in which but *two*
of the Narragansetts were spared to carry back the
tale of insult and defeat. A band of warriors was
straightway sent up to avenge their brethren, but
were again forced to quail before the arrows of the
entrenched and triumphant Nipmucks, and retired
from the field, leaving their dead behind them. The
bodies of the slain were interred in deep pits at the
junction of the Quinebaug and Assawaga rivers, a
spot still known as "the Indian Burying Ground,"
in Danielson, where many Indian relics have been
unearthed. The name Aspinock, designating the
Quinebaug valley near Lake Mashapaug, is transla-
ted by J. Hammond Trumbull—"an eating place,"
and may have received its name from this encounter,
which surviving Nipmucks detailed to the first white
settlers. The Narragansetts would doubtless have
given a very different version.

After settlement by the whites, and particularly
after the Uncas claim to Mohegan and Wabbaquasset
countries had been allowed by the Government of
Connecticut, the Narragansetts found it difficult to
maintain their footing within Connecticut lines.
Moosup, alias Pessacus, a war-like chieftain, brother

12

to Miantonomo, affixed his name to the largest branch
of the Quinebaug, and struggled manfully to retain
the Quinebaug country now included in the towns of
Plainfield and Canterbury, but according to Roger
Williams, in 1668, the Nipmucks had then for a long
time renounced allegiance to the Narragansetts, and
the border-land between Connecticut and Rhode
Island was but a patch of ground, full of troublesome
inhabitants, sandy, stony, and scarce worth fighting
for.   During King Philip's war these inhabitants
sought shelter at the headquarters of their respective
tribes, and the barren patch was made more waste
by ravages of roving bands, carrying off all the corn
and swine that could be found therein.   Its first white
Providence visitants were a company under Capt.
Nathaniel Thomas, who scoured the country far and
wide in pursuit of the fugitive King Philip.   The
night of August 3, 1675, they reached the second fort
in the Nipmuck country, called by the Indians—Wap-
o-sosh-e-quash—Wabbaquasset, a mile west of the
present Woodstock Hill.   Capt. Thomas reports—" a
very good inland country, well watered with rivers
and brooks: special good land, great quantities of
special good corn and beans, and stately wigwams as
I never saw the like."   These wigwams were built
under the direction of one of the Apostle Elliott's
Indian preachers, Sampson, and bear striking testimony to the success of his faithful labors.

Within ten years after the visit of Capt. Thomas
and the close of the war the fertile fields of Wabbaquasset had been appropriated by our sharp-sighted
sister, Massachusetts, and a flourishing colony from
Roxbury had planted the town of Woodstock.
Though bound by ties of allegiance and blood to
Boston, these Woodstock settlers soon found themselves drawn to the nearer market at Providence,
and one of their first public acts, after formal town
organization, was a vote "To be at the charge of
making a way unto the cedar swamp on the other
side of the Quinebaug River for a road to Providence—Benjamin Sabin to do the work and Peter
Aspinwall if he can't do it." Our friend Peter accomplished the work in the course of a few years,
making a narrow way suitable for foot or horseback
travel. The greater part of this way ran through
the outlands of the distant town, as yet a barren wilderness, with only here and there the cabin of some
hardy pioneer, furnishing food and shelter for man
and beast.

As Pomfret, Killingly, and other Connecticut
towns struggled into being, they too claimed the
privilege of better communication with Providence,
and selectmen from the new towns joined with those
of Woodstock in petitioning Providence town council to help at their end of the work. Committees
from Killingly, Pomfret, and Woodstock were chosen

to meet at sun an hour high, October 3, 1710, "To
state a place over the Quinebaug River most commo-
dious for a bridge to meet the prospective highway,"
but ten years passed before road or bridge was accomplished.   The southerly towns gained first the
right of way.   Travel from Norwich and Windham
passed through Plainfield over the "old Greenwich
Path," an Indian trail " trod out " by early Narragansett claimants.

   The General Assembly of Rhode Island and Providence Plantations met this need by voting in 1711,
that a highway should be laid out through Providence, Warwick, and West Greenwich to Plainfield.
Representations were made to the General Assembly
of Connecticut that travelers to the westward from
Boston and Providence, met with great difficulty and
were exposed to great danger for want of a suitable
country road through Plainfield and on to the colony.   The famous journal of Madam Knight, 1704,
gives a most graphic picture of the condition of the
roads, and the discomforts experienced in traveling
from Boston to New York, through Connecticut and
the Narragansett Country at that date.   Our colony
promptly responded to Rhode Island's suggestion.
A committee was appointed; land was freely given
by Plainfield proprietors, and a good and sufficient
causeway was constructed four rods wide and eight
rods wide at intervals for the convenience of loaded

carts in passing each other. A safe and sufficient
bridge was thrown over the Moosup, and canoes provided for transit over the turbulent and formidable
Quinebaug. This improved and convenient highway
became a popular thoroughfare, greatly facilitating
communication between Boston and Providence and
New York, called the best and nearest route that had
then been opened between those business centres,
and aiding much in the development of these towns
and the intervening country. Eastern Connecticut
now found in Providence her nearest market and
base of supplies. The boundary quarrel that raged
so fiercely in the vicinity of Pawcatuck river was
confined to southern sections, and pleasant, neighborly intercourse was constantly maintained between
Windham, Plainfield, and Canterbury settlers and
their favorite market town.

The northerly road, through Pomfret and Killingly, was much behind time in construction, mainly
because it was carried through by the towns apart
from Government aid. Peter Aspinwall's bridle-path
was long the only means of communication, even
barrels of rum having to be brought up on horse-
back lashed on trees and dragged behind the rider.
The road was finally accomplished under the super-
vision of Nathaniel Sessions, of Pomfret, who drove
the first cart over it to Providence in 1721. His son,
Darius, future deputy-governor of Rhode Island,

12*

then ten years old, may be said figuratively to have
driven in the last spike—the youngster claiming the
honor of conducting the oxen into the town. In the
following year the long-coveted bridge was placed
over the Quinebaug at the High Falls (now in Putnam) by Capt. John Sabin.

.With these two important thoroughfares open to
the public, intercourse between the inhabitants of the
neighboring colonies became more and more frequent
and friendly. Heavy carts laden with country produce; horse-back riders with pillion and saddle-bag;
foot-travelers with packs, way worn and weary, were
ever passing to and fro. Hartford might be the
political centre of these Connecticut towns, but
Providence drew them by the stronger ties of business
relations and social affinities.

And yet from the outset there was a radical difference between a Rhode Islander and a Connecticut
man. The Rhode Islander affected white corn; a
golden yellow was the true hue for Connecticut. A
Rhode Islander might go to church and build a house
of worship if he fancied—the Connecticut man was
compelled by law to build a meeting-house and go to
meeting. It is a little amusing to read in some local
town history the glorifications over these " good men
who in their own poverty and scarceness made immediate provision for public worship, &c." Of course
they did this, and in the majority of cases did it freely

and heartily, and yet the truth remains that the law compelled them to do it, and they risked the loss of their township by failure. Woodstock, unable by the difficulties of Sir Edward Andros' administration to build their house and settle a minister promptly, felt constrained to make most humble acknowledgment for being in some respects "out of capacity;" and beg the General Court "that the great overturns that had been might excuse this omission." The patent of Killingly, granted in 1708, expressly provided "That no person now inhabiting on said land, or any other persons dwelling without this colonie who have purchased any lands within the said township, that shall not give due obedience to all the laws of the colonie for the upholding the worship of God paying of all public charges shall have no benefit by this act." The redundance of negatives makes this injunction more emphatic.

Trained from infancy to consider the stated establishment of religious worship as the first and chief duty of state and town Government, it is not surprising that our Windham County visitors and sojourners should be scandalized and grieved at Rhode Island's destitution. As this lack of ministers and meeting-houses became more apparent with increasing intercourse, their hearts were moved to missionary efforts in their behalf, and in 1722, the year that the Quinebaug bridge was erected, a petition was

sent to the General Assembly of Connecticut, praying
that a brief might be granted in several congregations, gathering contributions from such as were
piously inclined towards introducing and carrying on
the ministry of the Gospel in the town of Providence.
The Governor and Council graciously granted this
request and a brief was sent out, directed to minister or
deacon of a number of eastern Connecticut churches,
including those in Windham, Canterbury, Plainfield,
Pomfret, and Killingly, empowering them to make
collection for this purpose. This missionary movement in behalf of benighted Providence. had been
set on foot by some zealous ministers of Massachusetts, who addressed a letter to the deputy-governor
and other eminent men of Providence, in which, after
commending the peace and love with which religious
societies of different modes of worship had been
entertained in Rhode Island, and the freedom and
safety they had enjoyed in preaching, they most
humbly begged their countenance and encouragement if it should come to pass that a small meeting-
house should be built in their town to entertain such
as are willing to hear our ministers. Deacon Jonathan
Sprague's reply to this humble request fairly makes
our ears tingle. Genuine Rhode Island *sauce* has a
very pungent quality.   .

In spite of this rebuff a Congregational meeting-
house was built on the corner of College and Benefit

streets, and served for many years as a beacon of Puritan orthodoxy among the Baptists, Quakers, and Independents of free-thinking Rhode Island.

With passable roads and suitable provision for Sabbath-keeping, emigration to Providence assumed a more permanent character. Young men averse to farming found employment in other lines of labor. Boys went to sea and found places in stores. Enterprising young men of better education, like Darius Sessions, tried their chances in the growing town. Some went back in time for the girls they left behind them. Others found wives in their new home. An elaborate entry in Thompson church records, in mammoth letters, with the blackest of ink, records the marriage, 30 September, 1739, of Capt. Nicholas Cook of Providence, to Mrs. Hannah Sabin, daughter of Capt. Hezekiah Sabin, first settler of Thompson Hill, and proprietor of its famous old red tavern in the centre of the common. As the bride was only eighteen we may assume that this honorary title was given her out of respect for the dignity of her own and her husband's social position, or, perhaps, with a prophetic sense of the honors that awaited her as the wife of a governor and mother of a dozen stalwart Rhode Islanders.

Capt. Sabin's successor in the tavern was a typical Rhode Islander, Benjamin Wilkinson, one of the class of roving Yankees described by Washington

Irving, whose idea of settlement in life is to set out
upon his rambles. It is said that he kept tavern in
every stand between Providence and Connecticut's
north-east corner.   When he brought up against
Massachusetts line, on a beautiful farm west of the
Quinebaug—now in New Boston—people thought he
had come to stay, but destiny met him in the shape
of a shabby old traveler who carelessly asked what
he would take for the premises.   Mr. Wilkinson
named a high figure and thought no more of it till
in a few weeks the shabby old man appeared before
him with a bag-full of gold and silver ready to clinch
the bargain.   Amused at the incident, and always
ready for travel, Mr. Wilkinson resigned the farm
and purchased the tavern stand on Thompson Hill,
where his energies found ample exercise.   He hauled
off the stones, dug out aboriginal tree stumps, and
planted peach-stones by every rock and along the
highway for public accommodation.   Through all
his wanderings he carried with him Rhode Island
ideas and white seed corn, and while serving as
committee for the standing society and opening his
house to accommodate the Congregationalists in winter, he gave sympathy and building spot to the struggling Baptists.   On one occasion only he came into
collision with church authorities—that fatal Sunday
when a *grind-stone* was heard in his door-yard, just
across the road from the meeting-house, creaking

rustily through all the services. A deputation of worthies was sent to remonstrate with the offender. Mr. Wilkinson promptly denied the charge. "But we hear it now," persisted the complainants. "See for yourself," retorted the smiling landlord, pointing out to the committee a pair of Guinea fowl, the first brought into the town and yet untrained in the strictness of Connecticut Sabbath-keeping, whose doleful croak, aggravated by homesickness, had subjected their owner to such reproach and visitation.

It was probably through Mr. Wilkinson's effective influence that a new business interest developed in the north-east town of the county. The first public attempt to trade with Providence was through a peculiar local institution known as "the Butter-cart," which ran about the town from house to house like the later peddler's cart, picking up such small products as housewives could spare, and bringing back in exchange those minor luxuries that husbands too often overlooked or refused to purchase. A small nutmeg cost a ninepence in those days, and as for pins, a single paper was considered a life-long supply. Stories are told of mothers bringing up a large family on four rows, and grandmothers exhibiting with pride the "great pins" that had formed a part of their bridal outfit. The "Butter-cart" was held in high esteem by wives and daughters, and its arrival and departure looked for with as much interest as if it bore the treasures of the Indies.

In the hands of Mr. Wilkinson's son-in-law, Daniel
Larned, and his partner, John Mason, this primitive
barter-trade expanded into a great commercial enterprise. A store was opened under the Great Elm,
South Neighborhood, filled with all manner of tempt-
ing West India goods and useful articles. Carts
were sent all over the country, picking up marketa-
ble products. Ashes were taken in for the extrac-
tion of potash and pearlash, pork and beef were
prepared and packed for market; a shop was added
for nail manufacture—all to be exchanged for West
India goods in Providence—especially those most
needful and desirable articles—rum and molasses.
The arrival of the first hogshead of the latter article
at "Larned and Mason's store" was made a day of
special festivity—boys being allowed for the first
time to revel unstinted in the favorite juvenile dainty
of the period—hot roasted potatoes smothered in
panfuls of molasses, and crammed all sizzling and
dripping down the throats of the happy urchins.
The candy of later days was far less positive in flavor.

The close of the French and Indian war was followed by a season of great commercial and maritime
prosperity, shared alike by town and country. Business enterprises like this in Thompson were not unusual. Samuel McClellan, of Woodstock, engaged in
this domestic and foreign traffic. The country village
was in process of evolution. Store and shop were

added to the small knot of dwelling-houses cluster-
ing about the hill-top meeting-house and tavern.
The out-lying district first included within the limits of Providence township was now set off into
the separate towns of Cranston, Glocester, Scituate,
Smithfield. The great highways leading through
them to Providence were more and more thronged
with travelers and traffic. Substantial bridges over
the Quinebaug had long replaced the primitive
canoes. Taverns were in great force in those days
of slow traveling and fast drinking. Eaton's tavern
in Plainfield was now a famous place of resort and
entertainment. The constant stream of travel made
it very difficult to keep these roads and bridges in
suitable repair. The need of better roads was vo-
ciferously argued in town meeting and General Assembly. Special orders relating to their renewal and
maintenance were promulgated by both Governments.
Plainfield and Canterbury were particularly bur-
thened by highway demands and charges. In fact
the road-question was one of perennial agitation.
The first mail carrier of whom we hear was Thomas
Mumford, who carried the mail once a week on horse-
back to New London. The first public conveyance
passing through Windham County was a weekly
stage coach running from Providence to Norwich, in
the summer of 1768. Mr. S. Thurber reports the
first chaise-jaunt in 1776, when, after all the labor

13

bestowed upon it, the road was so stony and rough
that he could not ride out of a slow walk, and was
near two days in going to Pomfret. Dr. Stiles, of
Newport, future president of Yale College, makes
statistical notes of his many journeys over the Providence road, which unfortunately give little more than
date and distances. " From Uncle Abel's (Woodstock) to Browns of Killingly, 8 miles: thence to
Larneds' store, 2 miles: thence to Woodstock, 7 miles ;
from Uncles' to Wilmots, 17 miles : from Woodstock
to Providence, 34 miles : from Pomfret to Providence,
36 miles. Expenses at Prov. 3 shillings: at Foster's,
3s 3d : at Larned's, 5s 3d "—which shows that a great
man may make a very dry record.

Among the reciprocal interchanges between Providence and Windham County we have to include crimi-
nals and refugees. The honored names of Stephen
Hopkins, Resolved Waterman, William Rhodes, and
other compassionate and large-hearted Rhode Islanders, appear upon a petition in behalf of the notorious Dr. Hallowell, who had " fled his country "
upon conviction of criminal offence. An exile, destitute of everything but want and misery, he begged
permission to return to an unhappy wife and seven
unfortunate children, " who not participating in the
guilt had too deeply tasted of the punishment."
Fine and imprisonment alone he could have borne,
but to sit upon the gallows with a rope around his

neck, suffer public whipping and further punishment
at the pleasure of the court, was thought by Dr.
Hallowell and his Rhode Island sympathizers to be
more than the laws of God did, or those of men
should, inflict upon human offenders. Providence
sent a noted refugee in John Aplin, an Englishman
of learning and good address, who acquired a hand-
some estate by legal practice, but it being discovered
that he had received fees from the opposing parties
in an important case, "between two days fled his
country" and found refuge in Plainfield. It need
hardly be said that such refugees as were driven
from home on charge of heretical or heterodox opinions, were received with open arms by the sister colony. The Rev. John Bass, who was dismissed from
the Congregational church of Ashford "for dissent-
ing from the Calvinistic sense of the quinquarticular
points," was welcomed to the pastorate of the First
Congregational church of Providence, upon the decease of its first pastor, Rev. Josiah Cotton. Rev.
David Rowland of Plainfield, who had been made
for a dozen years a bone of contention in that town,
the church refusing to let him go and the town withholding his salary, found peaceful anchorage in the
same church after the death of Mr. Bass. In place
of writs, attachments, and noisy controversy, we are
told by the newspaper of the day, December, 1767—
that "young ladies, daughters of Liberty and indus-

try, met at Mr. Rowland's with their spinning
wheels, and at night presented him with *1,020 knots*
of thread."

The troubles with England, the shadow of approaching war, only made the intercourse between
Providence and Windham County more intimate and
continuous. Hitherto the tide of emigration had
run eastward—now a reflex tide brought many worthy
families to permanent establishment in Windham
County. The Stamp Act excitement sent Godfrey
Malbone, of Newport, to Brooklyn Parish, where he
attempted something like the old Narragansett style
of living with his three-thousand-acre farm, his scores
of slaves, and church of his own order. But the
great body of new-comers were families of moderate
circumstances, who preferred to cultivate their farms
and bring up their children apart from sea-board
alarm and agitation. Chase, Congdon, Fisk, Bul-
lock, Jackson, Hoppin, Randall, Thompson, Torrey,
Tourtellotte, Wheaton, are among the many Rhode
Island names thus engrafted. Others came as transient residents.

But Windham County did more than furnish a welcome refuge during this long period of distress and
exposure. Perhaps her most noteworthy service
was furnishing the colony a deputy-governor in full
sympathy with patriotic sentiments and movements.
Darius Sessions had continued to advance in influ-

ence and position. In 1762 he was chosen assistant; in 1769 he became deputy-governor and indirectly afforded much aid and comfort to those inclined to resist British oppression. His wilful blindness in regard to the "Burning of the Gaspee," called out much amusement as well as criticism. As the aspect of affairs became more threatening, Gov. Sessions purchased a country-seat in Thompson Parish—the "old Joseph Cady house" and farm. The reconstructed mansion became a famous place of resort during the war, entertaining many a noted historic personage. Pres. Manning, who, during college suspension made frequent visits in Windham County, speaks with admiration of Gov. Sessions' excellent farm and superior accommodations. The meanderings of the good president give us glimpses of many of these new homes:

"Left Providence, Thursday, April 29, reached Col. Abraham Winsors, 10 miles; 80. Traveled to John Brown's farm at Chepachet 6 miles; refreshed and proceeded to Capt. Corliss's, Killingly 12; road extremely bad; visited Mr. Jones; set out after dinner and visited Gov. Sessions. After tea traveled to Benj. Thurbers in Pomfret, 6 miles; roads better. Sunday A. M. Preached at James Thurbers; lectured at B. Thurber's at 5 P. M. house crowded; audience very attentive and affected. Monday. Visited Paul Tew at Woodstock, also at Mr. Cahoons, Thompsons, B. Lindsleys. Tues. Visited Col. Nightingales, Pomfret, dined. He lives most elegantly; has a grand farm; entertains hospitably. Thence to Jeremiah Browns and Captain Bowles's, Ashford."

13*

Pres. Manning does not report to us the lasting effect of his preaching in Pomfret. From other sources we learn that it aroused so much interest that the Congregational minister, Mr. Putnam, became alarmed lest it should lead to the spread of Baptist principles, and that he challenged the president to a public discussion of the points at issue. But the ponderous town minister was no match either in oratory or argument for the college president, and the whole affair resulted in many conversions to Baptist principles and the formation of a Baptist church—a permanent memorial of the Revolutionary exodus. The keen eye of President Manning recognized peculiar facilities in Pomfret, and especially its favorable position for "a boy's school," which he hoped to have established there as a *feeder* for his university.

But Windham did even more than furnish farms and homes to her eastward neighbors. These were the days of Rhode Island's extremity. Her exposed position on the sea-board brought constant peril and invasion. Time and again the militia of Windham was summoned to her aid. Companies hurried down in the autumn of '76 on receiving news of an approaching fleet, but were too late to prevent the occupation of Rhode Island by a strong body of British troops. Windham County soldiers formed a part of the force retained for the defence of Providence, and aided in

the several attempts to dislodge the invaders. In
the stormy campaign of 1778 her services were especially valuable. The prospect of naval coöperation through the agency of the French fleet encouraged the patriots in their preparations for the
recovery of Newport and Rhode Island by a strong
movement on land. Powder, cartridges, provisions,
everything that could be spared, were hurried down
to Providence. Companies of militia and volunteers
marched off with renewed spirit and hope.

Here are three Thompson brothers tramping along
on the familiar road to Providence—stout young fellows who, having each served his lawful quota in
Connecticut, are bound to seek their fortune in
Rhode Island. They have packs on their backs, and
the youngest carries somewhere an inkhorn and a
roll of paper. Little Rhody is all astir these midsummer days. Men are marching off from every
hamlet and farm-house, and the women are getting
in the hay and doing all the farm work. One grand
effort is to be made to drive the British from Rhode
Island, and our youngsters are quickly snapped up
and drafted into service. Zeph's ready pen gives us
his experience, and takes us to the scene of action:

"August 5, 1778, drafted to serve on Rhode Island twenty
days ; got some cloth for a knapsack ; went to Jonathan Spragues
& got a good gun and cartridge, & then Jesse, John and I set out
together with some more from Job Angells. 6. Did march to

town and barrack in the Court House & so it goes. 7. As soon
as light got up & see the Continentals march for Tivertown;
got some breakfast at Mr. Trips; very warm—I went to the
New Light meeting-house & got a canteen, and about twelve we
set out for Tivertown; marched through Pawtucket, into See-
konk or Rehoboth, and did lie in a meadow on the side of a fence.
8. Mustered about 2 or 3 o'clock, & marched into Swanzea &
got a bowl of chocolate; and then over States Ferry into Free-
town & ate dinner & very hot, & then over Fall River into Tivertown & I encamped by side of a haystack. 9. Had bowl of
chocolate & went to Parade & fixed our guns for business; then
rode over the ferry & landed upon Rhode Island; formed &
marched up to the Fort & laid down in the great chamber 10.
French did engage the English batteries with their ships and
cannonaded very smart for 8 hours, and Jesse & John went to
the lines scouting at night. I went upon guard to the bridge &
did sleep on the road."

And that night came on that terrible Norther that
drove the disabled French fleet far into the sea and
blasted all the fruits of careful preparation—one of
those fateful storms that again and again have
changed the course of human history. Our poor
Zeph gives his experience :

"11.   Jesse & John fixed a little wall to break the wind & we
have nothing to eat hardly. 12. Knocked about & built a stone
house and covered it with hay and it rained very hard & the
house leaked so we thought we could not stand it ; went about
a mile & got wet to the skin and found a haystack & almost
chilled to death we rolled off some hay & did lie by the stack &

were almost dead in the morning. 18. Crept out & came to
stone house, found John alive & after a while I got dry & had a
boil on my eye & did feel very poorly ; our folks fixed up our
barracks & got a little green corn & slept very well. 14. Got
up and paraded & marched to the water & fired in platoons. 15.
Not well, nor John either. All the brigades marched to the lines
& we got our packs brought down & encamped in a huckleberry
plain. I had a clean shirt and trousers & I felt very poorly ;
blind with one eye & not any tents ; nor haint had but the Heavens to cover us. 17. Still very poorly ; ate nothing. In the
late storm one or two died and several were chilled so that many
in our regiment are very unwell ; cloudy & foggy ever since we
came upon the Island.

    19. A little firing on both sides. 20. They fire a little ; are
all the time entrenching and building forts ; I wash my knapsack & feel some better. 21. Set out upon fatigue down the
lines ; had to dig in plain sight of the enemy ; the ground was
but just broken when they began to fire upon us very bad but
received no damage. 23. Enemy fired hot shells & we begun
the breast work for the great mortar. Jesse & John & I worked
till noon & placed the great mortar. 24. Constant firing. 25.
All paraded and went to headquarters ; went three miles for
rum. 26. Six or seven men killed ; an 18-pounder split all to
pieces & a brass mortar. 27. Paraded ; took our cooking uten-
sils & went to head-quarters & delivered them up, & marched
through Portsmouth to Bristol Ferry & went on board a vessel
& there was but little wind & that was wrong & we got along
slowly & beat along almost to Conanicut Point & cast anchor and
lay till light & then struck for Warwick Neck and landed and
came along and got a good breakfast of wheat bread and milk
and came through Pawtucket to Providence and Warwick into
Smithfield to old Father Job Angells & got some victuals & I

feel very poorly. Camp Middleton, Aug. 18, 1788." "Dec. 80,
was paid $69.00 for soldiering on Rhode Island."

With this service our friend's military service closes,
but the continued diary gives very realistic pictures
of every-day life in this transition period. Zeph remains in the vicinity of Providence, picking up work
wherever it can be found, digging stone, laying wall,
fiddling, and dancing. When work fails in the winter he and his brother tramp round the country like
young troubadours, dressing flax at farmers' houses
on shares, making brooms, splitting rails, and fiddling. Again in Rhode Island in summer, working
for Job Angell, Philip Sweet or Joseph Farman, running a farm for John Jenks, &c. Times are hard and
the value of money fluctuating. He buys a scythe
for $25.00, which he breaks in hanging; gives £59 48s
for winter suit of coat, jacket, and breeches of light-
colored cloth, and receives $81.00 for fiddling all
night at John Smith's raisers' husking. Work is di-
versified by frequent frolic and dances; have two fiddles at some huskings, and drink without measure,
for these were "high old times" in Rhode Island in
spite of war and poverty.

As years go on our hero takes more note of public
affairs. "March 6, 1781 Men gone to Newport for
one month; news of peace: Reformation in the
camp; Hear that fifteen tons of silver in French
horn-pipes have come to Boston. March 14. Gen.

Washington came into Providence from Newport. Sept. 14, 1782. This day died at Providence the Hon. Governor Cook (husband of our little Hannah Sabin.) March 31, 1783. A flag from New York says P. E. A. C. E ; handbills say 'Peace;' April 25. A proclamation of Peace this day."

Zeph takes to himself a Rhode Island wife and tries hard to gain a livelihood.   "June 16, 1784. Buy fifteen dozen cakes and liquor for Ordination Went to North Providence for Ordination and sold liquor and cakes and they danced all night." He fiddles at huskings and dances, but profitable work is hard to find. Times are still hard, and currency unsettled.

"June 24, 1788. Great rejoicings to-day on account of a new Constitution being framed and sent out to see if it will be ratified by the people. July 4. A great feast at Providence, they roast a whole ox. There are two parties here Federalists and Anti-federalists," and Zeph, a man of the people, sympathizes with the Anti party.

Intercourse between Providence and Windham County becomes more lively with development of the new nation. "Thurber & Chandler" return from Pomfret to reopen their store near Major Thayer's tavern with its appropriate sign—"The Bunch of Grapes." Here they not only dispensed West India and New England rum, and French brandy on the most reasonable terms, but " woolen and cotton hand-

cards " of their own manufacture. It would be impossible to give anything like a complete list of the
young men from Windham County now seeking work
and business openings in Providence. And at the
same date one of its leading merchants, Col. William Russell, is establishing a potash manufactory in
Woodstock—buying up land, constructing extensive
works, experimenting upon " Hopkin's Plan."

In educational matters there was equal reciprocity.

As during the war Plainfield academy had proved
a boon and refuge to many a Providence youth, num-
bering among its graduates such future celebrities as
Nicholas Brown, Henry Wheaton, Wilkins Updike,
so now Windham County in turn sent her sons to
enjoy the privileges of Brown University. The first
Windham County name that appears on her lists
is William McClellan of Woodstock, 1782. Other
Windham County boys, graduating before 1800, are
Wm. Wilkinson, Jacob Converse, James B. Mason,
George Larned, Peleg Chandler, Joseph Eaton, Eras-
tus Larned, Philip Hayward, Wm. H. Sabin, Alvin
Underwood, Nathan F. Dixon, Judah McClellan,
Lucius Bolles. Wm. Wilkinson while conducting a
preparatory Latin school served as college librarian.
Hon. Darius Sessions, John Mason, James B. Mason,
Lucius Bolles, appear among the university trustees.
A much respected citizen of Woodstock, Dea. Jesse
Bolles, served faithfully as steward and registrar.

The traditions of college life, as handed down by some of these early students, show full participation in the frolicsome spirit of the day. Everybody has heard how the president's cow was decoyed into the belfry, but how nearly the youngsters succeeded in *hanging* a negro boy after a mock trial is one of the stories that had better be left to Carlyle's "wise oblivion." The standard of scholarship, as compared with that of later date, was extremely low.

Good fellowship and genial hospitality were characteristic traits of that period. The frolic element, so prominent in Zeph's circle, pervaded all classes. Between the families who had removed from Providence and their town relatives, between new comers and country cousins left behind, were continuous social interchanges. Pomfret, with its historic "Pucker Street," became an early place of resort for Providence aristocracy, its Episcopal church and fashionable assemblies giving tone to its society. A future governor of Rhode Island, Nehemiah Knight, residing for a time as business agent at the Quinebaug Falls—now in Putnam—was extremely popular among the country belles, and is accredited with the honor of instituting the picnic in Windham County, and also of providing a place for it, laying out a walk on the tongue of land between the Quinebaug and Mill rivers, under the fanciful name of La Solitaire.

With all this skurrying to and fro, on horseback

14

or with cart and chaise, the roads, according to Dr.
Dwight, were in a very unsatisfactory condition, due
to the unconquerable spirit of its inhabitants, who
insisted that free-born Rhode Islanders ought never
to submit to the tyranny of compulsory church rates
or turnpike fare. The sum grudgingly allowed by
legislature only sufficed to keep the road repaired
in the vicinity of Providence. But the law of progress asserted itself in time and by 1805 roads were
completed connecting with a number of turnpikes
established in Windham County, and "free-born
Rhode Islanders," says President Dwight, "bowed
their necks to the slavery of traveling on a good
road." The Providence and Springfield Turnpike
passed over Thompson Hill. Another in the south
part of Thompson ran through Woodstock and Ashford to Somers, on the north line of Connecticut.
Still another crossed over Killingly Hill to Pomfret.
A very important thoroughfare—constructed by the
Connecticut and Rhode Island Turnpike Company—
passed through Killingly and Brooklyn, connecting
with Boston and New York Turnpike. And the old
road through Sterling and Plainfield was managed
by another turnpike company.

Windham County could not have carried through
all this road-making but for the simultaneous development of manufacturing interests. A wonderful
spirit of enterprise dawned with the new century.

Little Rhody led the race in manufactures, but her energy and capital surpassed the extent of her territory. The fraternal intercourse with Windham County was now turned to good account, and Windham's convenient mill-privileges were quickly appropriated by Providence capitalists. The second cotton factory by date in Connecticut, and the first in character and influence, was the well-known Pomfret Factory, with Smith Wilkinson for manager. Other privileges were secured in Killingly, Plainfield, Sterling, Thompson, and later at Willimantic. The list of Windham County factory owners includes many of the prominent business men of Providence. Reciprocal benefits resulted from these interchanges. The stimulus to energy and invention, the demand for labor and farm produce, the remuneration offered to men, women, and children brought new life to the country town. Laboring men with large families hastened to avail themselves of this business opening. Children rejoiced to tend the shining machines and pronounced them "the prettiest things in the world." And as all that was done in the mills in those days was to spin yarn to be woven on hand looms, this opportunity to earn money for themselves was eagerly welcomed by thousands of country women, unconsciously taking the first step in woman's emancipation in receiving personal pay for their own labor. Wives and daughters of merchants, lawyers, as well as of

well-to-do farmers, did not disdain to enter their
looms to weave cloth for Pomfret Factory.

This grateful boon happily coincided with new demands for money. Missionary movements were in
the air and many benevolent societies were in process of evolution. A brilliant daughter of Providence, Martha Whitman—wife of William H. Mason
of Thompson—took the lead in organizing a " United
Female Tract Society of Killingly and Thompson,"
borrowing for a model a very elaborate constitution
just adopted by the pioneer " Female Tract Society
of Providence."

The stewardship of Brown University passed from
Dea. Bolles to another son of Windham County,
Joseph Cady of Killingly. As the chief office of the
steward of that date was to furnish the commons
table for a crowd of hungry students, it is said that
Mr. Cady owed his election to office to the excellence
of his wife's cooking, as tested through their experience in keeping tavern on Pomfret Street. The
scale of prices is worth recording, in contrast to present charges—for lodging, six cents a night; meals,
super-excellent, twelve cents each. Mrs. Cady's reputation for good cookery was fully sustained at Providence, though it was hinted that her husband was
more successful in catering than in discipline. His
successor in office—another Windham County man,
Mr. Lemuel Elliott of Thompson—combined every

essential quality, and is still held in honor as the model steward of Brown University. Here again the wife (of course a Windham County girl) comes to the front, the superior quality of her *apple-pies*, as reported by an experienced critic, Mr. Amasa Mason, securing the favor of the trustees. The wisdom of their choice was abundantly justified. The departments of finance, cookery, and discipline were equally well administered. Mr. Elliott sat in state at the head of the ample board—a true " Autocrat of the Breakfast Table "—one tap of his carving knife usually preserving order. But if any youth indulged in immoderate effervescence the autocrat's strong grasp quickly set him outside the window. The savor of the Sunday morning breakfast of cod-fish cakes and raised biscuit, long lingered in the memory of Brown graduates. Mr. Elliott's term of service was prolonged from 1826 to 1864—during which period he was held in high esteem by students, faculty and general public. Windham may well take pride in the somewhat remarkable fact that for more than sixty years this important office was held by natives of our county.

The turnpikes, so opportunely opened, facilitated the needful interchange of cotton and store goods in the manufacturing era, and stage lines accommodated roads and factories. These were the golden days of the historic stage-coach, that delightful institution

14*

which some of us still tenderly remember. Punctual
as the sun, at 9 o'clock in the morning the Providence stage cheered my youthful vision, soon to be
followed by two enormous loads of cotton-bales,
each drawn by four stalwart horses. Four stages
passed daily over Thompson Hill, and at least the
same number over the Killingly and Plainfield routes.
Jolly tavern stands, at stated intervals, supplied all
needful entertainment for man and beast, and no
ascetic temperance legislation restrained the flow
of liquor. The barrel of beer was always on tap,
and the poker kept red-hot for flip-making. Could
anything have been pleasanter than a first visit to
Providence in one of these stage-coaches! The
ruddy, genial driver, John Wilkinson, perhaps, or
some kindred worthy, receiving you into his care
with paternal interest. What opportunity the long
drive afforded for friendship, flirtation and political
discussion.   Perhaps some magnate boarded the
coach, Smith Wilkinson or Sampson Almy, to be
remembered through a life-time. What family histories were made known to us as we jolted along.
Here was a youth with his bundle, receiving his
mother's parting counsel as he went out into the
world, or a brisk young girl alights, all ribbons and
finery, flush with her first earnings in the factory.
And then the bundles, messages, reproaches, picked
up along the way. We seem admitted into the pri-

vate history of every family on the road. Short
seems the five or six hours' journey as we rattle over
the pavement of Weybosset and Westminster—and
our country eyes open widely at the array of stores,
the throngs of well-dressed people, and all the won-
ders of the city. The Arcade especially excites our
wondering admiration, and we marvel at the pre-
sumption of our country villages in attempting to
pattern that magnificent structure.

This manufacturing and stage-coach era was one
of steady growth and healthy development. Providence was transformed from a provincial town to a
flourishing city; the Windham County towns made
very solid gains in population and equipment. Some
of Rhode Island's peculiar institutions were transplanted to her neighbor's territory, viz.: two Quaker
meetings and meeting-houses, and a Quaker boarding-school. And while Providence boys were avail-
ing themselves of the privileges of Plainfield Academy and Black Hill Boarding-school, a Providence
mother removed to Pomfret—Mrs. Mary Vinton—
was training her own boys for positions of high
honor and usefulness in army, church, and state.
Windham County boys were more and more drawn
to Brown University. Among the bright lights sent
by her to Providence during this period were Abraham Payne, of Canterbury, who won a high place at
the bar, and George W. Danielson, of Killingly,

editor of *The Providence Journal.* The number of
Windham County men engaging in business and en-
rolled among her honorable merchants is quite beyond our estimate, while to keep the balance, Watson,
Tingley, Nightingale, and Morse were added to the
list of Windham County manufacturers.

A notable feature of the closing years of the turnpike era was the bridal processions gaily wending
their way to Windham County. Connecticut, for once
less rigid than Rhode Island, tied the nuptial knot
after one legal publishment of marriage intentions.

Three successive Sundays, or at least fifteen days'
notice was required by the sterner law of Rhode
Island. Thompson, just over the line, was especially
favored by these votaries of Hymen or "Weddingers,"
as they were commonly called. For a time these
ceremonies were performed Sunday intermission by
the ministers, who read the brief publishment of
marriage intentions at the morning service, but the
number of hymeneal visitors became so great, and
the consequent Sabbath-breaking so alarming, that
they resigned the lucrative office to Capt. Stiles, the
veteran tavern-keeper—who was made justice for this
especial service. A man of commanding presence,
with a melodious voice and very impressive manner,
he performed the ceremony with remarkable grace
and unction. Many a Rhode Island family dates its
genesis from the old Stiles Tavern of Thompson. An

occasional runaway with irate father in hot pursuit
added to the interest of these matrimonial visitations,
which made Thompson and its landlord almost rival
Gretna Green and its blacksmith.

In striking contrast to these blissful cavalcades
was the band of wearied fugitives who appeared on
Thompson Hill one June morning in 1843—the flying
remnant of Dorr's disbanded army—crushed by the
ruthless hand of "Law and Order." That any permanent result should follow this invasion curiously
illustrates the beneficial tendency of Providence and
Windham County intercourse.   Accompanying or
following the main body was one of the leaders of
the rebellion—Aaron White—a lawyer of good standing and more than average ability.   Anchoring at
the "Old Barnes Tavern," just on the line between
Connecticut and Massachusetts, he decided to make
his home in that vicinity, and as one dead to his
former life he proceeded at once to select a burial
spot and compose a Latin epitaph, which thus trans-
lated he ordered inscribed upon his grave stone :

> " In memory of Aaron, son of Aaron and
> Mary White, born Oct. 18, 1798,
> Here driven into exile
> While defending the rights of man,
> I found Hospitality and Love,
> A Home and a Sepulchre."

In his subsequent life, prolonged over forty years,

Esquire White practiced law as occasion offered, and amused himself with the study and collection of coins, leaving at his decease four and a half tons of pennies which were valued at some $8,000. He left, by will, to the treasurers of the eight counties of Connecticut a thousand dollars each as a trust fund "for the procurement and maintenance of County Bar Libraries in their several County Court Houses, for the sole use of the judges and clerks of the Courts therein, members of the Bar and their students." It is certainly a very remarkable occurrence that a fugitive from the laws of one State should confer so great a benefit upon the law expounders and administrators of a sister commonwealth.

We have thus traced the intercourse between Providence and Windham County in all its varying phases —by Indian trail and " trod out " path, by bridle path and cart path, by turnpike and stage-coach, to the beginning of our own era. Great are the changes wrought in this last half-century. Old times have passed and all things have become new. One puff of the steam-engine blew down our turnpike gates. Railroad train and bicycle have displaced the stage-coach, and coming electrics cast shadows before.

Yet, as amid all the changes of the past these sections maintained such pleasant and helpful intercourse, even so under present dispensations. That artificial, almost invisible, boundary line which sets

them in different governments has never impaired
the interchange of friendly feeling and kindly offices.
History they say is prone to repeat itself.   As in
the very first beginnings of historic tradition we saw
our Nipmuck residents repairing to Narragansett
shores for a shell-fish treat, so now our Windham
people flock to the Bay for clam-bake and shore dinner.   And our Narragansett friends come in even
greater numbers to Windham County towns to find
—not lamprey eels alone—but her pure air, her
breezy hills, healthy and wholesome social influences.

VI.

A LIFE'S RECORD.

1777-1843.

Better than tradition, better than fact received
from ordinary historic sources, is the contempo-
raneous record, the living word, jotted down at the
occurrence of what it depictures. Hawthorne tells
us that even old newspapers and almanacs are "bits
of magic looking-glass, with the image of the vanished century in them." And still more vividly realistic is the family letter, the daily self-revealing journal, bringing us into living, personal relations with
human beings long passed from earth. Fortunately
for the world this custom of diary-keeping was very
much in vogue before the development of the personal element in newspapers, and has contributed
most essentially to our right understanding of many
facts connected with the early history of New
England colonies. Our indebtedness to Winthrop,
Mather, Sewall, and other chroniclers is gratefully
acknowledged. Many private, personal diaries are
constantly coming to light, giving us new insight
into political, military, ministerial, and secular affairs.

Some of them are from men of high official position. Ministers and college students were especially addicted to this exercise, and many phases of colonial and early national life are thus brought to intimate knowledge.

The journal on which this "life record" is founded is from a humbler source, a farmer's son with very limited advantages, and might be said to represent the daily life of an average Connecticut citizen during the period. It was kept by the same young fellow who gave us pictures of the Rhode Island campaign of 1778. He began it the previous year when ambling back to camp after a furlough, and continued it till near the close of his long life. Jotting from day to day the doings and happenings that came to pass, he gives us not only his own life's experience, but a fair transcript of the growth and development of the nation in whose birth he had borne a part. A musty pile of yellow foolscap, tattered ciphering and account books, tells the long story. Let us see what we can glean from it.

Dec. 3. 1777. We see a stout lad of eighteen riding leisurely over the hills of Windham County, on his way back to Danbury. Brothers John and Jesse enlisted into the regular State regiments and served their quota. Our Zeph, with a little more snap, or spring, or wilfulness, elects a different service. He has not very pronounced ideas about the true in-

15

wardness of the war that is in progress, but he likes
to be about "hosses," and appreciates the fun of
hunting Tories, and so he strayed down to Fairfield
County and enlisted as a teamster. He has already
spent six months guarding and carting Government
stores, and now returns to duty after a brief furlough.
It takes four days to reach his destination. First
night—"Put up at a very good tavern in Coventry."

Slowly surmounting the Bolton Ridges he spends
the second night at "old Captain Coles" in Farmington. On in the rain through Washington to one
John Clemmons in Litchfield.

"6. Through New Milford and Newbury and got
to Danbury about dusk."

Work begins next day, care of oxen and horses,
and foraging for supplies. Danbury was one of the
most important store-houses maintained by the Continental Army. The previous April through the
great "Tryon raid" it had sustained a terrible loss,
eight hundred barrels each of beef, pork, and flour.
Seventeen hundred tents, all burned and wasted.
Now they were struggling to replace these stores and
our Zeph drives all over the country with cart and
oxen—goes to Bethel, Stamford, Norwalk—"Stays at
a bad place. The man was clever but had a devil for
a wife." "Dec. 21. Went over a dreadful bad mountain into Duchess County to Col. Vandeboro's, and
loaded seven barrels of flour: went for hay to Joseph

Hanford's farm—a Tory that has gone to the Regulars."

It is all work and no play for our country lad. He complains of poor living; has no cook and no time to cook for himself; no bed to sleep in, no letters from home. How little this poor little teamster realizes the significance of what he is doing? How little he knows of what is passing? There is Putnam and his Connecticut regiments right over against them in the Highlands; Washington and his hungry soldiers at Valley Forge; Congress vainly striving to meet the situation; State Legislatures and Corresponding Committees at their wit's end for men and munitions, and our poor home-sick Zeph sees nothing but his small trials. Even Thanksgiving day " brings no rest."

Jan. 1, 1788. Prospects brighter. We get a cook and fare better. " Pecks folks are diabolical Tories but Mother Peck baked rye and injun bread for us Continentals and gave us a good New Years supper, rice pudding and baked beef—but the brandy is almost gone and what *shall* we do?" Feb. 2. Saw two of his neighbors and heard from home; first time since leaving it. A visit to Fairfield was another treat, for there he saw his brothers and " got a good dinner of scallops, pork-sides and bread." " Bought twelve sheets of paper and an almanac for a dollar: saw a lady with a roll upon her head seven inches high. It looked big enough for a horse and had wool enough in it for a pair of stockings."

At the close of the year, Zeph made over his oxen and rejoiced in freedom. "Nobody shall say when I shall drive team." He takes a job of flax-dressing upon shares; had good cider and a bed to sleep on. Spring comes on early; snipes whistle, frogs peep, but his year's pay is withheld, and then work fails him. He sells his horse for eight dollars, and that is soon eaten. Home-sickness sets in. He sees blue-birds, robins, black-birds, and tries "to fly home" after them like a foolish boy. Then he swallows his pride and goes back to teaming—"pities Continental oxen." A harder trial awaits him; his trousers give out. He could get no cloth for new ones or for patching. "My breeches, O my breeches," he bewails, and finally is reduced "to put on a petticoat." Among all the privations endured by Revolutionary soldiers, this was the most humiliating. And just at this time Capt. Hoyt's house is burnt down, and Zeph's knapsack is consumed with all his worldly goods, viz.—two canteens, one inkhorn and box of wafers, one gimlet, one pair shoes, one case bottle of West India rum, forty-nine pounds flax, one frock.

"April 22. Fast throughout Continental Army; did no work & drew butter for the whole month, eat victuals now at the school house and lie at Major Gailors on a feather bed. Take care of sixteen horses.

25. Bought cloth for breeches. Gay! Straddled two horses at once and run them till I fell through and hurt myself. 29. O, I hant got no breeches yet but today boiled or washed cloth to make some" and next day they were made and donned.

Various diversions were now practicable, such as raiding houses and mills for suspected Tories—and at the end of three months Zeph received wages and discharge, and gladly started homeward with a fellow freedman—"Through Woodbury and Waterbury, over the mountain through Southington to Farmington, Hartford, Bolton, Coventry, Ashford." Reached home at sun two hours high, a pleasant tramp in the freshness of youth and June.

Four days at home, one spent in "training at the meeting-house," and our restless youth sets out for Providence with his brothers. There are younger boys to help the old folks carry on the Bleakridge farm, and the older ones must work their own way in the world. Zeph finds work at low wages till drafted for military service. For these are stirring times. With the French fleet outside the Bar, and La Fayette and Green in counsel with Sullivan, and all the regiments that can be mustered in, and companies of militia, hurrying to Rhode Island for a desperate effort to drive away the British, these stout young fellows must do their part. Zeph's hard experience has been already given.

15*

A few days' rest at home followed the campaign,
when he called upon "the girls" and once more
"went to meeting in the meeting-house," and then
Zeph resumed work in the vicinity of Providence,
digging stones, laying wall, &c. Home at Thanksgiving time when a dance was on hand. He hears
of the death of one of the expected company—
"Benoni Smith—the ground caved in while he was
digging out above, and next day the jury sat upon
him and there was a dance that night and I went,
which at the time I did not think it was a fit season;
funeral next day."

Zeph did other things in those irrepressible days
discreetly veiled from prying eyes in undecypherable
hieroglyphics, for work was scarce and Satan pro-
portionately active. Fiddling and flax-dressing were
resources in the winter, when he and brother John
tramped about Connecticut, and found a job far over
in Cheshire—where they lived well and had plenty of
cider and good company. On good days they could
dress as high as fifty-two pounds—half of which was
their own—and on bad days cut rails and make
brooms with true Yankee faculty.

Again in '79 they seek work and fortune in Smithfield. Times are hard and currency all "out of joint."
Zeph gives fifty-five dollars for a ready-made linen
shirt, and pays for other needfuls in proportion. The
winter following was emphatically the *hard* one when

sickness and suffering prevailed alike at camp and at home. Walking home in January, 1780, Zeph is caught in the great snow-storm, struggles through waist-deep to a farm-house, where he spends the night. Next day by carrying a bushel of corn two miles to mill on his shoulders, he purchases a pair "of wooden shoes or rackets," which did good service through the snowy winter. Towards spring, on snow-shoes, he again sought for flax-dressing, but luck and work now failed him.

Resuming wall laying in Smithfield he records a strange phenomenon:

"May 19, 1780. Now let not this day be forgot. In the morning it was cloudy and we laid a little wall, wind southwest. About ten o'clock it looked darker and I expected it would rain and it grew darker and darker. We worked at the wall till we could not see to range ten rods right. We went into the house and it was about twelve. The fire shined like night. They light a candle to eat dinner. The air or clouds look like brass, yellow, and things too I reckon. 20. Last night was as much darker than usual as the day but I saw it not: was asleep."

Zeph's interest in meteorological observation was quite in advance of his generation. With keen eye he notes the changes of the weather, the direction of the wind, the coming and going of birds, the putting forth of buds. "Sept. 25, 1780. I see a star plain as

the sun right over head at mid-day." He sees it day
after day. " It rises some time before day very large
and bright."

Star-gazing in those days alternates with sky-lark-
ing. Zeph is in great demand for frolics and huskings, and handles the fiddle-bow as deftly as the
crow-bar. Still the hieroglyphics continue and multiply, hinting at some feminine complication. In
frequent visits at Bleakridge they become more vo-
ciferous. The course of true love is not running
smoothly. Finally a crisis is reached and Zeph
breaks out into open lamentations. He waits upon
somebody to a ball but is almost crazy. He can't eat
nor sleep and don't know what to do with himself.

> ·· Talks of louping o'er a lynn."

Other youth have survived similar mischances.
Zeph raves and tears in prescribed fashion, and then
takes himself back to work in Rhode Island ; has his
" hair braided the new braid " and starts anew.

Business and public doings now receive more attention. Zeph and brother John hire a farm and
carry it on together, with pretty sister Mary for
housekeeper. Men go to Newport for a month, and
Gen. Washington passes through Providence and
we try hard to get a peep at him. Still the times are
no better, hard work and poor pay is the cry. " I
pay sixty dollars for an ink-horn, also buy a sailor
jacket for self and a red broad-cloth cloak for sister

Mary." In spite of hard times the young folks have a merry season. "Who can say that former days were better than the present?" What a state of society is depicted in these yellow pages. What frolicking, and junketing, and promiscuous intercourse among these young people. How many children came into the world without, or quickly following, marriage of parents. Statistical Zeph apparently chuckles over these unseemly entries. "A baby laid to such a fellow," is no rarity in these pages.

After two years' hard work the farm is given up and wall-laying resumed, with intervals of haying and husking. Peace was proclaimed April, 1783, and we are hoping for better times—" When an honest man can live by the sweat of his brow, Sir."

Hieroglyphics appear again in which L. B. conspicuously figures—" L. B. and I rode down to Brown's farm and did eat and drink—watermelons plenty." And then comes the crowning entry.

" Oct. 14, 1783. Finished Farnam's wall; had Jonathan Angel's horse and rode home; then took George Streeter's horse and L. B. and rode to Elder Mitchell's in the evening, and about 9 o'clock we were married and so we rode back again, and two better beasts than we rode are seldom to be found, Sir, your most obedient. And Elder Mitchell was 85 years old. Oct. 15. Rode to Angels and Streeters and dug stone." Next month the young couple get

things together for housekeeping, and ride to Connecticut to keep Thanksgiving with old Father
Jacob, and appear out at church in Priest Russell's
meeting-house, and Zeph's fiddle is brought into
exercise.

And now, with wife and family to support, our
Zeph is busier than ever. He tries various schemes,
Yankee fashion; speculates in poultry; works " at
slaughtering ;" runs a meat-cart; sells liquor and
cakes at North Providence ordination, and then falls
back upon wall-laying. Husks and fiddles all night
through the autumn. Hires " two rooms up stairs
and one bed-room, half garret, needful cellar-room "
for twelve silver dollars rentage. But times are hard
and even this low rent is paid with difficulty. Children come on apace. A cradle is one of the first articles of furniture, and a " little lad " is soon trotting
round and tumbling down stairs. Then comes another boy, and last " our daughter Dolly."

And now come several hard years for our journalist. He finds that life is something more than a
frolic. He works hard in various ways but can hardly
make a living. There is the same cry all through the
States, and men are flocking to the new countries.
Twice our Zeph breaks away, axe in hand—the first
time for Whitestown on the Mohawk, and is sent
back by a rumor of small-pox. Again the next year,
1787, he trudges up to the Berkshire Hills ; visits old

Uncle Gideon ; looks round ; but his heart fails him and he sneaks back home—"a long journey and no profit to anybody, but 'tis past and cannot be recalled." Dec. 27, pays his taxes ; owes fifteen shillings and has nothing in the world but his head and a cow. Gets very little work through the winter ; neighbors sicken and die and there is "no one to assist in trouble." "A child found on Mowry's farm supposed to have been murdered." The fiddle is sold and frolicking comes to an end.

But there are brighter days in store for the young Republic. Willing and skillful hands will not always labor for a mere pittance. Those straggling, struggling, debt-burdened infant States are to be bound together into a compact *Nation* with central government and financial basis. Little Rhody, with all her intense individualism and assertion of State rights, has to submit to manifest destiny and overwhelming public opinion. Zeph chronicles the rejoicings "on account of the new constitution being framed and sent out," and the barbecue July 4, 1788, when "they roast a whole ox," but his sympathies are with the "Governor and Gen. West who are anti-federalists" —and anti-federal ideas stick to him through life.

With renewed hope he hires another farm this same spring, with two oxen, ten sheep, six cows ; but after two years has to borrow money to square up accounts with his landlord. Perhaps the good condition of

the family, as set down by statistical Zeph, March,
1790, has something to do with this failure. They
must have consumed much store of Rhode Island
pork and white corn meal. Zeph weighs two hundred
pounds; Mrs. Zeph, one hundred and ninety; Primus, seventy-nine; Jack, seventy-three; Dolly, sixty-
seven.

After many failures and vexations he hires a large
farm at halves and pitches into work more vigorously
than ever. He has sixteen cows, four oxen, and other
stock in proportion; hires two stout boys for six
months for $38 each. Wife and children help in pick-
ing up apples and other fruit, with one hundred and
twenty barrels of cider and forty-six barrels of beer
as the result of their labor. There is no hint of
church-going and Sabbath-keeping, but the children
go to school and are supplied with the new spelling-
book—"Webster make," and busy Zeph manages to
get time "to hear the scholars say their pieces."
Fourteen men help about the fall husking, and six
hogs are dressed, weighing 1,787 pounds. Free-
handed Zeph pays his help forty shillings more than
the bargain in return "for eight months faithful service." "Rafting thatch" for some of his buildings,
Zeph has a narrow escape: loses his footing, goes
down under the water, and sticks fast in the mud.
Two men, clutching him by the arm, are not able to
stir him till others pried him out with a haypole. "I

did breathe three times while under the water," but
got home alive, " thanks be to God," and we rejoice
in this ejaculation.

"Work, work, work," goes on with unabated vigor.
Another great crop of apples is transmuted into beer
and cider ; and cheese, butter, and pork, turned out
in heavy bulk. But with all this labor there is little
real profit. The great fruit farm, so near to Providence, draws a superabundance of company. Married sons and daughters of the owner flock thither
in and out of season, and the house is filled with
company and confusion. The children fall ill from
lack of care and accommodations, and Zeph and his
wife tire of their hard bargain.

And now old Father Jacob comes to the rescue.
Doubtless his faithful old heart had long yearned
over his Rhode Island prodigal, and now he opens
home and farm to him. The other children are out
in the world, and a place is ready for him—"Come
back to the good land of yellow corn and steady
habits, come back to church-going and town-meet-
ing, come back from Egypt to Canaan!" and Zeph
has sense enough to heed the call.

"April 1, 1796. Sat up all night and wife too, to
fix things to move." He went out alone with his fiddle-bow, and came back with a goodly caravan—wife,
three children, household goods, and a small herd of
cattle. Yet after years of hard toil he left debts be-

hind him, and confides to his journal that he owned
nothing but a small stock of furniture.

With old-time versatility Zeph adapts himself to
the situation, attends town-meetings, school-meet-
ings, trainings, ordinations, and funerals. For meet-
ing-going he has lost his relish, and the Rhode Island wife " cares for none of these things." His
energy finds outlet beyond the narrow farm routine ;
he picks up ashes and experiments in potash-making,
hires a saw-mill and gets out boards. With hard
work he achieves 344 pounds of potash, which he
carts to Providence and ships to New York, receiving ninety dollars cash in return. Another venture
brought him an hundred dollars. Yes, our Zeph is
getting on at last and settling down into an order-
loving, Connecticut citizen, with a little more snap
to him than common. Soon he is made "school
committee-man" for his district, and "went to Taun-
ton and hired a schoolmaster for four months for
forty-one dollars." Then, too, his politics are in his
favor. These Bleakridge farmers sniff at the stiff-
necked orthodoxy of the old Federal leaders, and
welcome the new Jeffersonian doctrines as expounded
by our breezy Zeph, and he leads the small minority
that cast their votes for Thomas Jefferson.

He goes to Oxford to attend " the Artifillians Funeral," observed in honor of Gen. Washington, " that
worthy general, who died December 14, 1799." Again

and again he rides to Oxford to hear the noted Universalist, Hosea Ballou, whose preaching suits him better than that of the plain-speaking Baptists and Methodists who are active in his neighborhood. More deaths than births are now recorded ; more funerals than weddings. Those old Bleakridge settlers are dropping off. Uncle Bijah "fell into the fire and died when there was no one in the room." Ten years later his aged widow found dead on the ground two rods from the house—all right the night previous ; " got up and dressed and took her pail and staff and went out to the well ; slipt down, no one hearing her, and she perished in the cold snow and rain."

In spite of these inevitable shadows it is a happy time at the Breakridge farm. The old people are easy-going and cheerful, and the young folks merry and thriving. They go to school and church and singing-school, and have young company. The boys are getting helpful at farm-work. Dolly has grown up tall and comely—" A right smart girl," the neighbors say, "her father over again." "May 11, 1801. Dolly ketcht cold by wading in the river; has pain in her side," and herb-drink does not seem to help her. Spring work is driving, but this illness is more than all. Early in June she is attacked with violent pain in her head—is light-headed and full of pain. Doctors are called from far and near. Wise old Dr. Eaton from Dudley ; famous Dr. Hubbard from Pomfret

each with his saddle-bags and train of "apprentices."
Dr. Hubbard stays six hours with her but there is no
relief. It is the height of the busy season; haying
is coming on; the potash kettle breaks in the melting; hail-stones fall as large as an ounce ball; but
what are these things compared with Dolly's sickness? "I stay in the house all day and only turn
some hay : wife and I sit up all night. Dolly grows
weaker and has no sense at all—a sorrowful spectacle
to behold." "July 1. Very hot. Dolly grew weaker
every hour. I was up twice before 3 o'clock and then
O lamentable, at half past four July 2, the breath
left the body of our daughter Dolly. This morn
makes twenty-one days and nights that this poor girl
has had such an extreme pain in her head and a fever
almost burnt up. The Doctor calls it the Phrenitus
and then the Pubmatick fever. 3. Elder C. did
preach and the funeral attended this afternoon."

Work is resumed next day, hoeing and mowing.
Poor Zeph sees Dolly in his dreams; holds her in his
arms, "looking just as she did when a baby," and
then the name drops out from daily record. Primus
goes to high school in Dudley for a term and then
keeps school himself. Jack, our youngest boy, starts
out in the world to work on the Boston turnpike.

"May 8, 1802. Snowed all the afternoon. 9. Froze
hard enough to bear a horse; cold and dry; no
grass." Zeph and his wife drive on with work all

the same, and watch with their sick neighbors, for it
is a sickly season, dysentery prevailing, and many
die. Jack comes home from his summer's work
hearty and rugged, with a hundred dollars for his
father, besides what he keeps for himself. Zeph sets
out apple trees, improves his farm and helps on public occasions; takes both his boys to help raise a
frame for the new Baptist meeting-house, where a
hundred men gather, and they have dinner, supper,
and liquor enough for all. Trainings are common, too, where liquor flows in abundance. There
is a " General Training " at Woodstock—a great parade, ending in much confusion. The day being hot
" many did near faint. Very dark night, with thunder and lightning; many rode off the road; fell off
and got hurt; horses could not see." Fortunately
for Zeph "rum was most poisinous to him for some
years," and he quit drinking.

Politics are very lively at the time of Jefferson's
re-election, and Zeph proudly reports "sixteen Republican votes," with larger gains in prospect. Baptists and Methodists are coming out against the old
Federalists and Standing Order. In 1806 Zeph is
very active in carrying through a great Republican
Fourth of July celebration at the Centre. He helps
build a bower, arranges toasts, provides musicians.
A flaming Methodist leads in prayer, and a fervent
Baptist elder delivers the oration. Federals and
16*

orthodox look glum enough at the parade, while
Zeph goes home in triumph and reports ninety-six
Republican votes at the next election.

Other public matters claim attention—" a new road
to be laid over Bleakridge; schools to be looked
after." Zeph hires a school-ma'am to keep school
three months for five shillings a week, while Primus
gets twelve dollars a month for his services. Here
are some medical prescriptions for colds and swollen
face—" a sirup of dogwood, marshmallow, barberry,
tansy and wormwood boiled with rum and molasses
—Substitute red-briar for dogwood and barberry and
boil in spring water that runs to the north." Sometime during these years Primus marries, somewhat
against the approval of the parents, and "has a
daughter without much clatter," and Jack slips off
to live with his Uncle Abel.

As the family lessens, work and business increase.
There is progress in the air. The life and stir of the
new century and republic are reaching this remote
corner. The "factory" has come to stay. Great
mills for working up cotton are going up within a
few miles. Zeph hires a saw-mill to get out boards
for the buildings. Scarcely has he begun work when
he is caught in a freshet. "June 14, 1807. Rains all
day. 15. A very great flood indeed; so high was
never seen before by more than one foot; new bridge
carried away "—but by working and watching day

and night Zeph manages to save his mill. The next
year the road-making is resumed. Over seventy
men at work, with many oxen, plows, and carts.
Zeph leads with six men and four oxen, and furnishes
cider by the barrel, but again "contradiction and
dispute" block the wheels of progress, and the
needed road is left unfinished. With all his digging
and driving he is ready to help in sickness ; attends
the funeral of a neighbor's wife, and "the most people present I ever saw at a funeral." A little girl
neighbor, four or five years old, "got up in a cart
and jumped about, and fell over the foot-board, and
cries, 'I have killed myself,' and died in half an hour."
Zeph carries six to the grave in his big wagon.

"Sept. 15, 1808. Drove a wagon to Pomfret to
Regimental training, and carried four men for three-
and-sixpence each." Three days later and the big
wagon takes a load of eight "to hear the Methodists
at their first camp-meeting. They keep it five days
and nights. Oct. 14. Carry wool to be carded at
the Factory—Cut sausage meat and filled the skins
with a tin on purpose—a great improvement upon
stuffing it in by fingers."

"1809, March 4. James Madison takes his seat as
president. Sept. 4. Raise in all a hundred and fifty
bushels of potatoes. Nov. 8. Father rather poorly.
12. Had a bad night, sat up in chair. 25. Father
worse, rather more weak and faint; sleeps most of

the day; fails fast. 26. Some above 8 o'clock my
father left this earthly tabernacle. 15. Rain; Elder
C. preaches; funeral set at 11, went to the grave at
3 P. M." The aged mother soon follows—"May 11,
1810. Mother very poorly. 22. Mother seemed in
more extremity, and left breathing a little after three.
Four of her nine children attend the funeral, where
Elder C. officiates as previously for Dolly and father."

And now Zeph is left with wife, work, and weather
observations. "1810, Jan. 14. The coldest day that
most ever was known," the "cold Friday" of mete-
orologic fame. "March 12. A great snow fifteen
inches deep." A school quarrel demands heroic
treatment. Zeph is one of three men chosen by the
district "to see what was to be done," and he "went
to the school inspectors and brought eight of them
down to the school house, where they heard all sides
and corrected both parties."

A new era opens this autumn of 1810. "I take
yarn from Pomfret Factory to weave." A great
opportunity has come to these suppressed New
England women. Weaving this smoothly-spun yarn
into cloth they receive good pay in any kind of goods
they fancy. How the tongues and shuttles rattle in
many a farm-house. Our friend, Mrs. Zeph, is one of
the first to improve the privilege. Everything else
gives place to the cloth weaving; even neighborly
calls and afternoon going-out-to-tea are suspended.

"I hope you read your Bible," hints Elder C. in one of his pastoral visitations. "Gracious," was the quick reply, "I don't git time to look in the alma-nik." Four pieces of heavy bed-tick are carried back to the Factory in December and broad-cloth taken in exchange. Then two tailoresses appear and exhibit for their week's work great coats for Mrs. Zeph and Jack, straight-body coats for Zeph and Jack, and two waistcoats, for which work each re-ceives one dollar and twenty-five cents. Yarn for seven hundred and fifty yards of bed-ticking is brought home for spring work, and while the "good wife plies the shuttle," her good man hires a grist mill for the season, and by help of fourteen oxen and as many men, set a new millstone. Another rebellion in the school-house is settled without outside inter-vention. "They could not turn out the master."

September, 1812. Zeph takes seven passengers for a dollar each to witness the brigade training at Brooklyn. He reports, "five regiments on parade, one of horse, twenty-five hundred troops, and four times as many spectators, something of a war-like appearance"—an exhibition calculated to rouse more interest in the war then in progress.

1813, June 21. Jack, now at home for the summer, is warned "to be at the Centre tavern complete in armor by twelve to go to New London as there were British there." Four neighbors' boys obeyed the same

summons, "most of the infantry and all the militia
that did not abscond," for this war is unpopular in
New England, and even Administration men like
Zeph and his neighbors have little enthusiasm. Those
that stood fire were marched into the meeting-house,
and treated to a spirited address from the minister
before starting on their march. Communications with
the outside world are still infrequent, and little was
heard from the absentees during their three weeks
service. The invasion was not accomplished, and the
boys had a good time and brought back, instead of
laurels, a list of false alarms, fizzles, and ridiculous
sayings and doings that made sport for a life-time.
Reports of naval victories enkindled war-like sympathies. "October 3. Hear that Commodore Perry
hath taken six British vessels on Lake Erie."

Elemental disturbances receive more specific record.
"February 10, 1814. Rains hard and froze on trees;
fore twelve at night trees began to break and split,
and the dreadfullest cracking that ever I heard. They
say it was like the report of heavy artillery. 11. The
trees bowed their heads like weeping willows, a
melancholy sight, and the fruit trees are broken as
the oldest man never saw before."

"1815, Jan. 31. Exceeding cold, coldest morning
for many years by the thermometer." The historic
September gale came the same year. "Rained very
fast; hard wind; between 9 and 10 A. M. began a

tornado; southeast wind blew very hard indeed; hath torn down thirty-seven large apple-trees, and upset many smaller ones; near all our fence torn down and timber lands most dreadfully turned up by the roots."

The cold summer of 1816, handed down by tradition as the "starved-to-death" summer—is duly and daily noted. "May 7. Windy and very cold. 17. Very cold. 29, 30. Very cold and dry with frost. June 4. Frost. 6. Very cold night, ice froze as hard as window glass; put up sheared sheep. 7. Very exceeding cold; wore coat, jacket, surtout, and wig, and none too hot. 10. A very hard frost, ice as thick as half a window glass; corn cut close to the ground." This condition prevailed through the entire season—cold and dry with a few warm days. Very cold spells in July, August, and September. Zeph harvests five loads of corn, "two good-for-nothing but fodder, only two bushels fully ripe."

"1817, Feb. 14. Caught in Providence by a cold snap exceeding anything that hath been in fifty years by the thermometer—warmed four times coming home; many froze some but I did not, coldest night most ever I see." Another cold spell came in May. "12. Cold night, ice on grass. 16. A very large black frost, exceeding cold. 20. Ice on grass-top like shot. 21, 22. Hard frosts."

These frost-bitten crops and war prices make hard

times for the poor, but Zeph is fore-handed now and
able to relieve needy neighbors, lending them money
and helping in many ways. Meanwhile the loom is
busy as ever, turning off great pieces of bed-tick,
gingham, and "dimino." "War's alarms" do not
disturb the peace of the old farm-house. Jack is
living at home now with a brisk, young wife—a
neighbor's daughter, very acceptable to the old folks,
and grandchildren are making the house merry.
Primus is plodding along steadily and has a houseful
of stout boys and girls, some of them always stopping at "Grandpa's." And there are hired men at
work on mill and farm, travelers stopping to chat,
townsmen discussing war and politics—a busy, cheerful, prosperous household, with Zeph for head and
centre.

"Feb. 14, 1815. Hear news of peace, *Peace!* 28.
Federalists celebrate P. E. A. C. E. between America
and England at the Centre, and there is a great ball
in the evening. March 4, 1817. James Monroe
takes the chair as president and David D. Tompkins
as vice-president." The war is over now, but there
is a battle going on in Connecticut; a fierce fight for
a new State constitution, and our Zeph is one of the
foremost fighters. They say he is captain there at
Bleakridge, and brings down loads of men in his big
wagon to town meeting. "Sept. 4. Went to Free-
man's meeting and the Republicans chose two Representatives to our liking; farmers; a good day."

"July 4, 1818. Went to town meeting to choose
delegates to send to Hartford to frame a constitution
for the State of Connecticut. Federalists had two
votes most. Sept. 29. Heard Constitution read."
A week later town accepted constitution by a vote of
174 versus 95, and Zeph is "well pleased." And now
the Republicans have control in the old Federal
town, and Zeph is selectman. His energy and versatility find ample scope in his new office. Now he
is letting out the poor to be boarded for a dollar or
seventy-five cents a week; or buying a new town
hearse; or laying out roads; or deliberating with
officers from other towns where to set the new court-
house. A special service is performed in perambu-
lating the boundary line between Massachusetts and
Connecticut, involving ten days labor. "July 5, 1819.
See the blazing star."

With increasing years and honors, Zeph manifests
greater zeal for public worship; owns two pews in
the Baptist meeting-house, and helps on repairs for
the same, and buying a farm for the minister. Ordinations, association meetings, baptisms, funerals, are
duly chronicled. A great "revival season" excites
much interest. Sees "Elder C. baptize seven of them
young girls, and hears two more tell the travail of
their minds; staid to see them take sacrament, home
at sundown." "April 5, 1820. See three dipt at Baptist meeting-house. June 14. Went to Baptist meet-

17

ing-house and heard a woman preach from Vermont
and she preached well, I thought too. 18. Went to
meeting and Elder C. he whipt us smart for hearing
a woman preach and I wish he had heard her himself." [It is said that Elder C. referred to this woman
preacher who had been allowed to occupy the pulpit
in his absence " as a grievous wolf who had entered
the fold."]

Common and uncommon casualties find place in
the record. A small fire starting by the roadside
"went up the hill as fast as a man could walk ; fought
fire as long as we could see ; next morn, rallied early
and fit fire to Alump Pond—thirty-four men. It ran
north a vast ways, cutting all before it."

"April, 1821. Neighbor M.'s died this day about
mid-day, sudden ; fell over backwards in her chair ;
taken up and said she was dying and it was so. June
20. Hard thunder shower, lightning struck powder
house. This clap struck down H. C., flung him down
lifeless, but he came to, was blue but full of pain.
Sept. 1. As hard a shower as ever I knew, filled up
streams like a freshet. 3. Strong S. E. wind and
rain, many trees blown down, fences and most of our
apples. 15. Down by the pond trod on a water-
snake, and it bit my leg, and it swelled and was sore.
Kept on working. 24. Leg no better, swollen more,
pain some. 25. Had a hen split open and put on my
leg three or four hours, then burdock leaves. 26.

Put on more leaves and went to see the regiment per-
form at the Centre. 28. Put meadow moss on leg
and it looks more purple. 29. Set out for Franklin
to see Dr. M. and he said he could cure the bite of a
snake, had poultice. 30. Another poultice and physic,
pills at night. Oct. 1. A wash and two pills. 2.
Physic and water gruel. 3. Leg looks better. 5. Had
bandage made and Dr. M. put it on. Paid Dr. M. ten
dollars for attendance and nearly five dollars for
board."

At home he resumes work, taking Dr. M.'s powders,
but the leg does not heal. All winter he is doctor-
ing and poulticing, and goes to see a man who had
been similarly afflicted by the sting of a wasp, but
gets no benefit. Finally he puts his case into the
hands of a "woman quack doctor," who, by various washes and treatments, succeeds in reducing the
inflammation, but he never regained his former
strength. That he should have survived the poison
and treatment shows great vitality. A neighbor,
who while cutting wood was called to go down into
his well for a bucket, was taken with great pain,
shivery, cold sweat, and died in twenty minutes.

March, 1826. Work is laid aside, and Zeph is
driving round buying store-cloth, a new hat and pair
of boots, and finally a *trunk*. What does this mean?
We look back along the crumpled page, and there,
half concealed by old-time hieroglyphics, we find the

key to the situation. The crowning honor of his life
has come—Zeph has been chosen town representative and is going to the legislature! Little did he
think when he tramped through the State fifty years
before, driving team and swingling flax, that he
should revisit those scenes in such honored guise and
company, driving in coach and four with fellow legislators. But these fifty years of life and work have
taken the spring and nonsense out of him, and it is
a somewhat sober old fellow that now drives over the
hills. "I feel neither smart nor courageous," is his
meek admission ; in fact he is homesick and out of
his element. He boards at "Widow Bishop's," and
sees a steamboat and other new things, and we may
be sure he never missed a roll-call, and voted the
straight party ticket. But one permanent effect came
from this New Haven sojourn. Among his fellow
boarders there was a glib Methodist minister who
walked and talked with our homesick legislator, and
somehow made clear to him some things that had
before puzzled him, perhaps those Calvinistic points
that have bothered wiser heads than his. However
that may be, Zeph joins a Methodist class after his
return, and slipping down to the river is quietly baptized one Sabbath summer evening.

The shadows lengthen. Zeph seems an older man
after his return from New Haven. The year of 1828
was especially calamitous. "A cow breaks her leg

and has to be killed; sad for the poor cow;" an ox
sickens and dies; the colt dies; it is a bad season
for lambs and sheep, and even the geese refuse to
hatch properly. Cut-worms appear in great force
and cut off the young blades of corn. June 30, a
hard thunder shower. Nathan's new house was
struck; the clock was torn to pieces, and a dog under the table killed; but a "deaf boy heard better
after the shock." And it is what old people call " a
very dying time, indeed." Neighbors and kindred
drop off like autumn leaves. One brother dies after
long illness; one is found dead on the road, supposed
to have fallen off his cart when asleep. Pretty sister
Mary, who kept house for us long ago in Rhode Island, comes from the West to visit her old home and
dies soon after her return. Sister Hannah, living
near by, soon follows. This neighbor wastes away
in long disease, Zeph and his wife watching with him
night after night, after their old, helpful fashion.
That one, going cross-lots through a wet place stumbled "and fell forward with his forehead against a
stone and his face in the water and died surprising." Another is drowned in his saw-mill flume.
Saddest of all was that of the lone, lorn woman found
dead in the swamp. It is supposed "she got up in
the night in a fright by the wind blowing very hard
and started for a neighbors but got out of her way
into the swamp where she fell. She left her shoes

and stockings in the house." Poor lone creature,
flying barefoot and panic struck to meet her death in
the dank swamp—does fiction parallel these trage-
dies of real life ?

But a new source of comfort has come to our old
journalist. Politics have lost much of their interest
with change of party names and measures. We are
Democrats now fighting Whigs, Banks, and Anti-
Masons, but not with the old fervor. There are
things of more vital interest upon the stage. These
are the days of " the great revivals of 1830–33," and
Zeph's whole heart is in the joyful work. Meetings
are held everywhere, at private houses and meeting-
houses; "pike-gate and grove." "See Elder T. baptize old Miss W. and many people." "Benjamin A's
son speaks like preaching, many more talk; a very
good meeting." "Elder Lovejoy is here, (a noted
name and preacher.) Two were plunged and two
more had water poured on their heads." "Aug.,
1830, went to meeting in a tent, 36 x 20—some speaking, no preaching; tent full and many more outside."
Camp meetings and " protracted meetings " are kept
up the following year, and Zeph reads his Bible
through by course in the interim, beginning January
1 and finishing March 31.

The clouds darken. The mother of the household,
the strong, bustling, hard-working wife and mother
is failing in strength, but the work goes on as usual

and the loom is seldom idle. Zeph, whose turn for rhyming gains upon him, sends this humorous missive to a neighbor :

> " My old dame is sick and poorly,
> And now there is more yarn yet lacking,
> She thought she'd state the matter fairly
> And have you bring the filling airly,
> And if you don't bring more blue than red
> You had better put yourself to bed,
> She hath been sick and kept a-drilling,
> And now hath stopped for want of filling."

But the trouble increases and becomes more manifest. Work can no longer stifle the growing anguish. Neighbors flock in apace ; sometimes ʻʻ six women at once." Poultices of every conceivable material, hot and cold, dry and liquid, are vainly applied. "Very full of pain," " wastes fast," are the discouraging entries. These are " solemn times " for our light-hearted Zeph. Three funerals reported in one day and things growing worse at home. " Sad, sad, sad." " Bad, bad, bad. A very bad day with some and I am sorrowful." But the illness was short. Worn with hard work and life's burdens the strong frame soon succumbs. "She fell a-bleeding, grew dark to her, faint, and she died just before twelve, Sept. 14, 1831, aged 73."

And now Zeph is left in the old home with Jack and his wife at the head of affairs. But he is still too

vigorous in mind and body to settle down into a
subordinate position, and public affairs claim attention. He superintends the work on the new school
house in *our* district, selects brick of the best material, and does the work so thoroughly that it still
bears witness to his fidelity. Then he builds a good
stone wall for our burying-ground, and pays his
heavy taxes for all these improvements without
grumbling.

"April 9, 1833. 'Tis said that I am seventy-four
years old this day, P. M. Thanks be to God that he
hath spared me so long." He has more time now to
note the weather and its changes. "We had an early
spring, robins, blue-birds and red-winged blackbirds
early in March. A hard frost in June killed most of
our corn to the ground; beans also;" enjoys in November the wonderful spectacle of "many shooting
stars." Meetings engross much time and interest.
Now some famous Methodist or Baptist elder gives
a rousing sermon; then they meet in some private
dwelling—"a glorious meeting without preaching,
many brethren speak and all to the Bible truth."
He is in great demand for funeral occasions as bearer
or manager this same Zeph who once danced all
night when a mate lay dead in his coffin. But he is
still Zeph, now "Old Zeph." No one would think of
calling him anything else, or know him by his family
name alone. He is a noted "character" now at town

meetings and all public doings, with his quaint old
wig and many-caped cloak, his reminiscences and
weather-saws, and his knack at rhyming. Asked to
make a rhyme upon an easy-going neighbor, more
fond of prayer meetings than work, he instantly re-
sponds:

> " There's Uncle Ase, so full of grace
> Sometimes his cup runs over ;
> He'll lay and sleep and let his sheep
> Eat up his neighbor's clover."

Or he pictures " a hired man " with one snap-shot:

> " Here's Joseph Pace with his long face
> And not so very fat:
> He's poor to hoe and worse to mow,
> And what do you think of that ?"

He has his old mare killed and buried decently,
which was twenty-seven years old :

> " She could not live on hay
> And I would not put her away."

" March 4, 1837. Martin Van Buren came in president. 5th. Sixty years past this day I went for two
months to drive a team for the Continentals, to carry
provision to the army at Peepskill; staid fifteen
months ; took team at Colchester. April 1. Town
meeting, chose George Nichols and Vernon Stiles
representatives. Republicans of the old stamp ; four

hundred voters in town. Some went not from this
hill but enough without them." Trainings have lost
attraction to him, perhaps because the trainings
themselves are not what they used to be, but he
takes little Nap to the Centre to see a caravan with
two lions and ninety-five horses.

Zeph works hard as ever, but there is a screw loose
somewhere, and the farm yields less profit. No more
carting surplus produce to market. No potash
making and mill-working, and factory-cloth weaving
under present administration. All the crops are
lighter, and there is hardly hay enough for the cattle.
The old man groans over this thriftlessness and " a
prevailing evil " at the root.

"April 9, 1839. Eighty years old this day & I am
poorly. A failing year in health and results of labor.
A severe winter, cold and stormy, no church going,
look after pigs and chickens and read good books.
Great excitement in town this spring of 1840. Fifty
new voters made "—737 votes cast. They say old
Democrats are ahead ; but they cannot check the
Tippecanoe craze and Harrison's election. Another
losing season is reported—" short in corn, rye, hay,
and so it goes."

Another cold winter keeps our friend at home, sinking more and more into the ordinary status of the
superannuated, and too often supernumerary, grandfather. The gay young fellow whistling over the

hills; the busy man of affairs driving about town
is gone, and we see a shriveled old man crawling
about the premises to feed the chickens, and poring
over Baxter's Saints' Rest and his Bible by the fire-
side. Friends of his youth, and companions of his
life have vanished. Public and even church affairs
no longer claim his attention. The great political
overthrow, the opening railroad, excite but a lan-
guid interest; but the journal begun in his youth,
the daily chronicle of life and weather, still remains
to him. Each morning, foul or fair, he hurries out
to breathe the pure air of Heaven, survey the sky,
note the direction of the wind. His dulled ear
catches the first song of the spring birds; his dimmed
eyes mark the springing grass, the swelling buds.
Two books are open to his fading vision—eternal
works and words, to which some mortal eyes are ever
closed. The great comet of 1843, stretching half
way across the visible heavens, thrills his old heart—
"but I go not to town meeting, nor to other meetings; have not strength for it."

The journal is getting mixed. The dates are jum-
bled up; we have turned the last leaf. "June 20,
1843. I find that I am failing; feel very slim." Still
the entries are kept up, but the lines run together.
The summer sun is shining in full strength; the corn
is hoed and the grass is ready for mowing, fully ripe.
The boys carry on the work—but old Zeph is "so

tired." July 26, he makes the last entry. A few more days and nights of weariness and watching and eternal rest is his. Good-bye, old Zeph. For more than three-score years we have traveled with you on your pilgrimage. Truly in thy case, "the end was better than the beginning." "Average Connecticut citizen" did we say? Faithful old soul; true to yourself, your country, and your God, well will it be with each if our record marks as high a figure.

VII.

DODGE, THE BABBLER.

In the closing years of the last century Pomfret
held a high place among Windham County towns.
Less in extent and population than most of its towns
it exceeded them in proportionate wealth and influence. It held the Probate office for the north part
of the county. Its post-office, administered by Judge
Lemuel Grosvenor, accommodated all the neighboring towns. Its leading citizens were remarkable for
sound judgment and intelligence. Perhaps that
United English Library, established as far back as
1739, had something to do with forming the character
of these men, and inciting young men to obtain the
privilege of college education. The town had also
been favored with a succession of distinguished
physicians. Doctors Lord and Warner, of Abington,
Dr. Waldo, of the Street, were noted in their profession, and Doctors Hall and Hubbard quite equalled
them in reputation and extended practice.

But perhaps there was nothing in which Pomfret
took greater pride than in her meeting-house and
ministers. This house of worship was the largest
and most pretentious in Windham County, and ex-

cited the envious admiration of other towns. Her
first minister, Rev. Ebenezer Williams, was considered
one of the leading ministers of his day, receiving by
bequest of Gov. Dudley, of Massachusetts, a memorial ring in token of esteem and favor. An incip-
ient wrangle at the time of building the great meeting-house was promptly healed by the suggestion
that lack of harmony might hinder them in settling
a minister, so that instead of having as they had done
the best of orthodox preaching, they might be compelled to take up with "New Light stuff," or some
inferior article. As successor of Mr. Williams they
agreed upon Aaron Putnam, a young graduate of
Harvard, who filled the place for many years to public
acceptance, a man of learning and piety ; a sound if
not eloquent preacher.

Mr. Putnam's unhappy failure of voice in the latter
part of his ministry brought in a new element. A colleague pastor was found needful, and again Harvard
furnished the candidate—Mr. Oliver Dodge. The
lively and agreeable manners of this young gentleman, and the freshness and animation of his discourses, won universal favor, and he soon received a -
unanimous call to the colleague pastorate, one person
only advising delay. But before the time fixed for
ordination, uneasiness had arisen. The spirits of the
young minister carried him beyond the ordinary
bounds of ministerial propriety, and unfavorable re-

ports came from abroad, so that the ordaining council was confronted by a small number of "aggrieved brethren," objecting to the ordination of the candidate on charges of "disregard of truth, neglect of duty, irreverent application of Scripture and unbecoming levity." Decision was referred to a special council of ministers and delegates—nine to be chosen by friends of Mr. Dodge, four by the opposition—which met in Pomfret, September 4, 1792. Four days were spent in considering the situation. The engaging manners of Mr. Dodge, and the large majority in his favor, pleaded strongly in his behalf; yet, as the good repute of a minister was a matter of such supreme importance, the council unanimously decided not to proceed to ordination. With paternal kindness they besought the young minister to accept this result in its true tenor, and endeavor in future to maintain that Christian spirit and live that exemplary life "that all the excellent and amiable talents and accomplishments with which God had been pleased to favor him, might be improved for eminent and most important purposes." Mr. Dodge demeaned himself through these trials with the utmost propriety, accepted the reproofs with due meekness, reflecting upon himself in several alleged instances except that of *falsehood* of which he had never been consciously guilty.

Uninfluenced by this decision, the friends of Mr.

Dodge proceeded to renew their call in a regular
society meeting, and requested the church to concur
in this invitation. Very great interest had now been
aroused, and it was evident that a large majority of
the church would vote in favor of settling Mr. Dodge.
To Mr. Putnam and the aggrieved brethren this
seemed a very injudicious and hazardous experiment.
There was one way by which this evil could be averted
—the power allowed to ministers in Saybrook Platform, by which their single vote nullified the unanimous vote of the church over which they were settled. Believing that Mr. Dodge was unfit for the
ministerial office, with a deep sense of his personal
and official responsibility in the matter, Mr. Putnam
now exercised this supreme power and dissolved the
meeting without permitting a vote upon the question.
So completely had a century of Saybrook Platform
administration eliminated from its adherents the
spirit of original Congregationalism and recognition
of the rights of individual church members, that this
act of Mr. Putnam's was fully sustained by brother
ministers. According to Windham County Association, the result would have been the same "had he
allowed the church to vote, as he would then have
left the meeting and rendered them incapable of
further action." That a large majority of the church
had any rights in the matter never seemed to occur
to them. "A few more than half makes no differ-

ence," said President Clap, of Yale. The rights of
majorities had not then been admitted.

But there was another side to the question. Opposition to the Saybrook Platform, initiated by the
unfortunate Separates half a century before, had
now been strengthened by more orderly bodies of
Christians. Baptists, Episcopalians, the newly-arrived Methodists, were equally averse to accepting
one religious denomination as the established church,
the "Standing Order" of Connecticut. Free-think-
ers of every shade were bitter against it. The spirit
of free inquiry was in the air. Public men who had
been active in the attainment of civil liberty were
realizing that religious restrictions were inconsistent
with a Republican form of Government. Foremost
among the opposers of the ecclesiastic establishment
of Connecticut was Zephaniah Swift, of Windham,
the able lawyer and jurist. His attitude on this
point had given great offence to the ministers of the
county who had upon this ground, opposed his election to Congress. Some of these ministers had assisted in the rejection of Mr. Dodge, and thus afforded
Judge Swift ample ground of retaliation.

As soon as the result of the Pomfret council was
given to the public, Judge Swift took the field as
champion of Mr. Dodge. The whole affair was "an
open attack upon religious liberty and the rights of
conscience." The power arrogated by the council was

18

"more unwarrantable and dangerous than that exercised by the pretended successors of St. Peter." The
act of Mr. Putnam "in nullifying the voice of the
church by his *single voice*, his *sovereign negative*, was
a most conspicuous instance of the arbitrary power
vested in ministers by that celebrated code of ecclesiastic jurisprudence, known by the singular appella-
tion of SAYBROOK PLATFORM." "Is the exercise of such
a power compatible with the equal rights, the unalien-
able birthright of man? Reason, common sense
and the Bible with united voice proclaim . . . .
that the CONSTITUTION which delegates to *one* the
power to negative the vote of all the rest, is SUBVER-
SIVE OF THE NATURAL RIGHTS OF MANKIND, AND REPUG-
NANT TO THE WORD OF GOD." Dodge himself was the
innocent victim of clerical revenge and malice; a
young man of superior genius and merit; a second
Luther, battling against ecclesiastic despotism."

Pomfret scarcely needed this outside stimulus to
self-assertion. Her sympathy, pride, and will were
all enlisted in behalf of the young minister. The
result led to immediate and great departure. A
large majority of members of the church withdrew
from connection, and proceeded to organize as "The
Reformed Christian Church and Congregation of
Pomfret." A satisfactory covenant was drawn up
and adopted, and public worship instituted in private mansions. Mr. Dodge, stimulated by contro-

versy and popular favor, was more eloquent and fascinating than ever. Crowds flocked to the new place
of worship, while the great meeting-house was almost deserted. Eleven male members, with their
families and minister, was all that was left of the
large church membership. The County Consociation, called to consider and advise, could do nothing.
The church had taken itself out of their jurisdiction
and Mr. Dodge scouted its summons to appear, and
declared himself "no more amenable to their control and jurisdiction than he was to the Bishop of
London."

Removed from all restriction, Mr. Dodge now came
out more openly as the apostle of a new dispensa-
tion. It was a time of great upheaval and discussion. Revolutions in Government and thought were
in progress. "The reign of long faces had passed;
ministers were now to act and talk like other men,
and unite with them in mirth, festivity, and amusement. Puritan blueness and austerity were to give
place to good fellowship and universal jollity. God
was best served by merry hearts and cheerful voices."
All knotty points of doctrine were to be ignored; the
Scriptures a sufficient rule of faith and practice according to each man's personal interpretation. In
the revolt from stiffened orthodoxy, these views and
practices as set forth by an engaging and eloquent
speaker were most attractive. Dodge was the hero

of the day ; the popular minister. Numbers united
with his church ; people from all the surrounding
towns flocked to hear him. The friends of free religion could not have selected a more eligible leader
than this clever and accomplished young man, who
could charm all hearts with religious rhapsodies, and
dance, drink, and joke with equal acceptance. That
it was difficult to find ministers of any standing to
assist in his ordination added zest to the situation, as
did the wordy battle in the columns of "The Windham Herald" between Judge Swift and sundry ministers who rushed to the defence of Mr. Putnam and
the council. Nothing in modern times equals the
bitterness of this newspaper controversy, and the
vituperations exchanged between the combatants.
All the sayings and doings of Mr. Dodge and his opponents were paraded before the public, and peaceful,
dignified Pomfret figured as the scene of this scandal
and division. Neighboring towns were drawn into
the strife. Mr. Dodge, by invitation of one of the
society committee, preached an afternoon lecture in
Woodstock meeting-house. The minister, Rev. Mr.
Lyman, having previously manifested his disapproval
went into the house during service and read a public
remonstrance. Whereupon the friends of Mr. Dodge
served a warrant upon Mr. Lyman for disturbing a
religious assembly, and compelled him to pay as high
a fine as the law would allow. In Pomfret the par-

tisan feeling became very strong and bitter. It entered into politics ; it divided families. The very
children in the street jeered and mocked at each
other as "Dodge-ites" and "Anti-Dodge-ites." An
opposer of the popular favorite lost his place as town
clerk, leaving this farewell upon Pomfret records :

"Here ends the services of a faithful servant of the public,
who was neglected for no other reason than because he *could not
Dodge* ≡≡≡≡≡ "

For more than six years this rupture and strife
continued, and Mr. Dodge maintained his prestige
and popularity. It does not appear that during this
period he lost ground or adherents. His " finely-
polished golden chain of equality and brotherly
love " satisfied his congregation ; his good fellowship
and easy insolence kept his hold in society. His occasional excesses and increasing levity were excused
as the exuberant overflow of spirits, and by his frank
admission of wrong. Nothing but his own suicidal
act could have lost him his place in heart and favor.
He held himself in restraint as long as it was possible and then gave way at once and forever. Everything was sacrificed for liberty in vicious indulgence.
After a week of revelry, driving from one low tavern
to another, and even offering blasphemous prayers in
a blacksmith's shop upon a challenge, he had the ef-
frontery to enter his pulpit and attempt to conduct

the usual Sabbath service. Rising to speak he fell
upon the pulpit overcome with drunken sickness, falling forever from his high estate. Apparently no attempt was made to excuse or palliate his conduct.
Of his large following not one was left him, because
he was too far gone to make the effort to retain them.
At a meeting of The Reformed Church of Pomfret,
July 4, 1799, upon complaint that Mr. Dodge had
been guilty of repeated instances of intemperance in
the use of spirituous liquor, and of indecent if not
profane language, it was voted that he " be excluded
from the rites and privileges of this church till by his
reformation and amendment of life he shall be again
restored to charity." But this charity was not called
into exercise. The " lost leader " gave himself up to
reckless dissipation. Seldom does one who has filled
so high a position, with so large a following, sink
into such sudden obscurity and oblivion. The Reformed Church vanished with its founder, its members gladly returning to the old church that welcomed
them into the fold. The name that had been so conspicuous dropped from the records and " Herald," and
he himself sunk out of sight and knowledge, only as
tradition whispered tales of " Pomfret's drunken minister."

But there is a sequel to the story. Last spring the
Probate judge of Windham at Willimantic chanced
to light upon a somewhat curious old document,

apparently an affidavit laid against a notorious offender, denominated "Dodge, the Babbler"—under date of 1805. The paper best tells its own story :

"Dodge, the Babbler, in an harangue at Glastonbury, on the 8th of August, 1805, after declaiming upon church & state & law and religion—exclaimed—

'God knows, angels know, saints know, all honest men know, the Devils know, and none but knaves and fools but what do know, there ought not to be any laws for the support of religion. We should not then see the poor man dragged to jail to pay a minister's tax, while his family were left starving : we should not then have to pay four or five hundred dollars a year for ministers' dinners at Hartford : we should not then see ministers have the privilege of turnpiking the road to Heaven and erecting gates and collecting tolls upon them.'

He also used this expression :

'Minister's salaries are a stink in God's nose, and a stench in his nostrils.'

The above expressions were heard by Mr. George Gilbert, of Hebron, and noted down at the time and in the meeting-house."

And so we see our brilliant young minister, who had stood so high in position and favor, who had been championed by Judge Swift and other distinguished advocates, wandering about the State as a mere "babbler" and driveler, undoubtedly injuring by intemperance and indecency the very cause of religious liberty that he was trying to advance—his abilities and opportunities wasted ; his life a wreck and beacon-warning. He is believed to have died in 1806—the year following this parting glimpse.

VIII.

OUR FIRST WOMAN ARTIST.

First in Connecticut, and in point of time one of
the first women in this country, to gain public recognition as an artist, was Miss Anne Hall, of Pomfret
and New York. She was only preceded and equaled
as far as we can ascertain by Misses Anna C. and
Sarah M. Peale, granddaughters of the distinguished
artist, Charles Wilson Peale. There may have been
local women artists in some of our large towns, but
none that gained more than a provincial reputation,
or were honored like Miss Hall by election to membership in The National Academy of Design.

Miss Anne Hall was no untrained phenomenon.
Like the Peale sisters she inherited artistic tenden-
cies. Her father, Dr. Jonathan Hall, of Pomfret, and
his father, had been lovers of art, and, unable to
gratify their own aspirations, were eager to foster
their manifestation in little Anne. Figures cut from
paper or moulded in wax at a very early age showed
great merit. A box of paints from China enabled her
to gratify her love for coloring and reproduce birds,
flowers, fruit, and whatever caught her childish fancy.

When a very young girl she accompanied an elder

sister to Newport, the home of the Mumfords, her
mother's family. Here she was permitted to take a
few lessons in oil painting and drawing from Mr.
Samuel King, the teacher of Malbone and Washington Allston. Mr. King also instructed her in the art
of applying color to ivory. Returning to her Pomfret home she practiced diligently in these various
lines, and had the privilege of further instruction in
New York city under the skillful teaching of Alexander Robinson, secretary of the Academy of Fine
Arts. With such opportunities for cultivating native
genius it is no wonder that Miss Hall achieved so
high a rank among the artists of her time. Her first
success was in copying from the old masters. Like
Hawthorne's Hilda she possessed that sympathetic
insight which enabled her to catch and reproduce the
very soul of the original. Her brother, Charles H.
Hall, of New York, supplied her with good pictures
to copy. Copies of Guido's pictures were executed
with a force and glow of coloring that won praise
from experienced critics.

In character and person Miss Hall was exceptionally
lovely—a bright and shining light in that cultured
society which distinguished Pomfret in the early part
of the century. A foreign visitor at one of her fashionable assemblies gave verdict—"That Miss Hall's
dress and demeanor would have done credit to any
court in Europe." She had the literary accomplish-

ments of her time, some of her poems long living in
remembrance. But above all she shone in beauty of
character—"her life a lofty striving after the highest
ideal, which she exemplified in every act and word."
Her ready kindness and sympathy, her willingness
to devote her artistic skill to memorials of departed
friends, was very noteworthy. Cherub faces of children long passed from earth are still held as priceless
treasures in many households.

But it was not till after her permanent removal to
New York city, about 1820, that Miss Hall's fame became fully established, especially in her chosen line
of miniature painting on ivory. Dunlap characterized
her work as of the first order, combining exquisite
ideality of design with beauty of coloring. He notes
especially her groups of children, "composed with
the taste and skill of a master, and the delicacy which
the female character can infuse into the works of
beauty beyond the reach of man." Some of these
groups received the rare compliment of being sent
abroad to be copied in enamel, and thus made inde-
structible. Miss Hall excelled in rich coloring, and
in those finishing touches that add so much charm—
flowers in the hands of her women, wreaths twined
about her cherub children, were marvels of grace and
beauty. Among many distinguished subjects, she
had the honor of painting one of the especial celebrities of the time—Garafilia Mohalbi. This lovely

Greek girl was taken captive during the war with the Turks, and ransomed in 1827 by a Boston merchant and brought to this country. It was this picture exhibited at the National Academy that brought Miss Hall her election to membership, and the engraved copy was widely known and admired. As market value in our practical days is often made a test of artistic merit, it may be noted that some of Miss Hall's groups were appraised at five hundred dollars, which was considered an extraordinary price for a native artist to receive.

Unaffected in character by her distinguished success, Miss Hall remained modest and retiring, never seeking praise or notoriety. Struggling artists from her native country gained ready access to her studio, and found her ready with sympathy and counsel. Our late artist, Mr. Sawyer, spoke of her with enthusiastic admiration, as one far in advance of the ordinary range of womanly attainment. She died at the home of her sister, Mrs. Henry Ward, New York, in 1863, having just passed her seventieth year. In the marvelous development of modern art, especially among women, this first woman artist in our State should not be overlooked, and it is hoped that a fitting memorial may sometime be prepared, with reproductions of those faces and groups which won such fame and favor.

IX.

JAPHETH IN SEARCH OF HIS FORE-
FATHERS.

It is not so many years since the great majority of
New England families outside of Boston were content
to trace a vague descent from one of "three brothers,"
who might have come out of the Ark, or the Mayflower, and then a genealogical boom swept through
the land, flooding it with family trees, charts, tablets,
genealogies, and histories. Various genealogic bureaus conducted by professional experts aid in the
prosecution of such researches, and testify to the
wide extent of the newly-awakened interest. With
such intelligent and sympathetic aid the inquirer can
hardly fail to exhume some eligible Pilgrim or Puritan
of approximate family name—a vigorous and fruit-
ful root from which he might safely predicate a
goodly family tree. But as he attempts to establish
connection between his own particular branch and
this primitive root, and trace out the various ramifi-
cations, difficulties multiply. If some eight or ten
branches shoot off into as many States, or, still worse,
if the off-shoots of two or three kindred roots com-

mingle in one town, he will soon be involved in inextricable jangle and confusion. Or if he be so fortunate as to trace his own lineage straight back to some ancient patriarch, there will be other branches missing, boughs lopped off, mysterious growths engrafted. The genealogist is sure to be confronted sooner or later with some obdurate sphinx of a problem, whose solution defies his utmost effort. The perplexities of Captain Marryat's hero in search of his lost father were light in comparison with those of our genealogical Japheths, searching through this great continent for their buried grandfathers and grandmothers. The friendly bureaus above referred to óften fail in such emergencies. They can furnish upon demand any number of reputable forefathers. It is for you to prove whether some particular specimen belongs to yourself, or to descendants of the other "two brothers." Left to himself the baffled Japheth pursues his weary search—exploring town and church records, unearthing family registers and letters, deciphering effaced epitaphs, afflicting the souls of far-off relatives by frantic efforts to make them bring to mind what they never knew or had long forgotten. Earnest appeals from some of these persistent searchers enlisted me in genealogical research. A dabbler in local history, it was easy for me to find and impart desired information. The exuberant and altogether disproportionate gratitude

called out by very trifling service in this line awoke
deep commiseration :

> " I've heard of hearts unkind, kinds deeds
>   With coldness still returning ;
>   Alas ! the gratitude of men
>   Hath oftener left me mourning."

How many snubs must have been endured to make
a little common courtesy so thank-worthy. Having
had occasion to solicit similar favors from strangers,
I answered every such appeal just as I liked my own
answered, and in following this golden rule worked
out a large experience which I would fain impart to
other wayworn Japheths still groping for lost grand-
sires.

And, first, I would premise for your comfort and
encouragement, that the object of your search *is* in
all probability attainable. Those exasperating old
ancestors and relatives, so persistently evading inquisition, did in very truth live and walk upon this earth
and doubtless left behind them some memorial of
their own birth and marriage, and those of their pu-
tative offspring. Your "missing link" lurks in some
furtive corner. That "pivotal fact" on which depends
your connection with the parent trunk, or the completeness and symmetry of the whole structure, is
safely hoarded by some obscure collateral, all uncon-
scious of the value of the latent treasure. In my

own experience the particular item establishing the
foundation fact of numerous investigations accrued
through the agency of a single individual, it might
almost seem providentially preserved to meet the
foreordained recipient of his fateful message.

Such was the Staytum case, involving a question
of locality. Descendants of the patriarch Samson
insisted that he settled at an early date on "the mile
square" east of the river in First Parish, which they
still held in possession ; but I found him an officer in
Second Parish, occupying a farm between two rivers
bounded by lines which human ingenuity could not
have made more crooked. It was perfectly evident
that the two farms could not have been identical, and
that a resident of First Parish would not have been
a church officer in the Second ; but the Staytums refused to yield an ell of their "mile square," or budge
an inch from their position in First Parish. A happy
chance opened communication with a ninety-year-old
descendant in a neighboring State, and from him
came positive evidence that the original Samson *did*
first buy and occupy an interval farm in Second Parish, and his *son Samson* was the purchaser and first
occupant of the "mile square." But if twenty surplus years had not been granted to the respected
Hezekiah my exhaustive arguments would have been
but vain words and fruitless Jeremiades. The genealogist may settle it in his mind as a primal axiom,

that one person and most probably *only* one on the face of the earth can give him definite information upon any controverted point. *One chance* in twelve or thirteen hundred million! But his inquiries are necessarily restricted to the Caucasian race, and finally narrow down to the sixty millions of the United States, and perhaps a few experts across the water. We might assume farther limitation by sectional probabilities but for the wide dispersion of descendants of early Pilgrims. Information concerning descendants of old Massachusetts and Connecticut families would be naturally sought in the vicinity of former places of residence, but you are quite as likely to find it west of the Rockies. Facts vainly sought in many native sources strayed back to me unsought from the Ohio and Mississippi valleys. I was long baffled in pursuit of a well-known Revolutionary veteran, very prominent at Bunker Hill and in subsequent service. Minute and persistent research in his own and neighboring towns failed to furnish any trace of him after the close of the war, and I finally numbered him among its unrecorded victims, buried like Moses in an unknown sepulchre, and then inadvertently stumbled upon his grave in the heart of the Empire State. A chance allusion from a casual correspondent led to the discovery of his early emigration and subsequent career.

[The preceding hints, written some years since, and

published in substance in the "New York Independent," require some modification to suit present conditions. During these years interest in genealogical researches has increased in geometrical proportion. Especially since the organization of the innumerable societies of "Dames," "Daughters," and "Sons," all requiring straight lines of descent, have these inquiries multiplied, and facilities for tracing these lines have increased in proportion. I should now discriminate between *roots* and *links*. The former are to be sought near the original settlements and landing-places. It is the connecting links that are often so evasive, and may be lighted upon in most unlikely places, and my "one man" theory should be restricted to inquiries of this nature.]

These opportune chances and unforeseen discoveries give a peculiar fascination to genealogical pursuit, rekindling in fossil sires the fires of youthful enthusiasm. That which to the uninitiated is a senseless groping among dead men's bones involves the tantalizing delight of gold-digging and treasure-hunting. Those thoughtless youngsters who jeer at genealogical enthusiasts might well envy the excitements and surprises of their adventurous quest. True, indeed, they are called to suffer many trials and disappointments. Nuggets are not found every day. Many a placer is dug over without disclosing one golden glimmer. The proverbial "hunting for a needle in a hay-mow" often typifies the experience

19

of the genealogist; yet, if the needle carry a *thread*
the chance is not so hopeless. The slightest clew
promptly followed; the tiniest atom of real gold-dust
may lead the way to marvelous' discovery. A mere
shred of a chance recovered my long-sought Missins.
A once prominent family, occupying a large tract of
land on a public thoroughfare, with a flourishing saw-
mill, a tavern, and roads leading to various settlements—not only had every vestige of them disap-
peared, but the site they had occupied could not be
identified. The oldest inhabitant had only heard of
them by vague tradition, and could give no satisfactory conjecture as to their place of habitation. I
spent days puzzling over the map for it. I set up
that saw-mill on every water privilege within the
territory, but try it where I would some condition
would be lacking; mill, tavern, highway, and by-
ways could not be made to fit in with appropriate
surroundings. Chancing at length to hear of an "old
Widow Missin," visiting in a neighboring town, I
hastened to call upon her. Like most women she
knew nothing whatever of "Mr. Missins'" family and
antecedents, but referred me to "Cousin Nimrod," in
some out-of-the-way neighborhood, as one who might
possibly give me some information. Starting next
day in pursuit of this mythical place and personage,
I drove some six miles southward for farther instruc-
tions, and then switched off into an old road winding

northeastward through pastures of scrub-oak and
huckleberry bushes, toward a bleak hill-range.
Having a well developed organ of what phrenologists
call "Locality," it was extremely harrowing to reach
a given point by describing the two long sides of a
very acute triangle, but when, after a wearisome pull
I reached the summit of the hill, all minor annoy-
ances vanished. For, oh, dear reader, I saw it all at
a glance. In this round-about style I had solved my
problem. Clear as a mathematical demonstration it
opened before me—the mill-stream and tavern-site in
the valley, the great highway winding round the base
of the hill, the old bridle-path eastward, and the
"trod-out path" behind me, that had led to this
happy outlook. Left behind by march of civilization
and change of business centres, enlocked by hill and
river, the lonely valley had evaded search till opened
by the pass-name of the *one man* who held the key
to its mysteries. The testimony of the faithful old
Nimrod confirmed local intuitions. A quaint old
hermit, forgotten by the world, alone he guarded the
Missin records and traditions. In this secluded nook,
once populous and full of life, his family had lived
and flourished for more than a hundred years, and he
alone could tell of their past glories, of the mill and
the great tavern, and seven gambrel-roofed houses
built for the seven sons of the first settler, and the
briary grave-yard where name and race were buried,

and then sent me home rejoicing by a cross-cut
across the base of my triangle.

Equally slight was the chance that restored to his
alma mater a certain shadowy James H. Goner, un-
heard of after his graduation early in the present
century. I take great pride in this achievement as
being myself the medium for recovering the trail and
enstarring the lost graduate among his fellows. The
dim *impression* of a surviving classmate, and a casual entry in some old class-book suggested Mytown
as his probable birthplace. Letters of inquiry were
sent to minister, town clerk, postmaster, &c., but as
the family had removed from town long before the
remembrance of any of these authorities no light
was gained from them. Catching at a straw, the college biographer next addressed the embryo town
historian, who with the rashness of inexperience essayed the quest. "It is of no use," sighed the maternal counselor so helpful in previous inquiries.
"I took special note in my young days of every
young man in town that was privileged with going
to college, and *never* was there a *Goner* among them."
Nevertheless a careful examination of the faded
church records detected a James Horner Goner baptized just in time for college entrance at the specified date. James H! First middle name on church
record! That *two* Goner families should have indulged in such extravagance when double names

were so uncommon was extremely doubtful, but admitting that the vanished collegiate was represented
in this record what chance was there of unraveling
his subsequent career, as his family migrated westward early in his college course and had long passed
out of knowledge. Well, it did look very dark for a
time, but gradually in the maternal consciousness
faint echoes were awakened of long-gone talk about
a "Goner wood-lot" left behind unsold till after the
death of the family head, when it was bought up by
"your Uncle Abishai," who had no end of trouble
hunting up the scattered heirs before he could secure a clear title. Uncle Abishai's papers and the
probate records furnished the missing link and evidence, enabling us to trace the fugitive to West Ten-
nessee, where he kept school, practiced law, married
and died, leaving a widow and several children to
receive his share of the Goner wood-lot.

[Another problem relating to this same Goner family has but recently attained solution. A somewhat
indefinite marriage record represented the head of a
large and respectable family as marrying "Susanna
Goner *alias* Fuller"—a way of putting it that was a
source of great perplexity to the present generation
of descendants. Whether she was a Goner by birth
or adoption could not be settled, and a "goner" she
remained for many years. But the increasing demand for Eastern ancestors at length brought inquiries from the long-gone Goners, and with them the

information that our mysterious Susanna was indeed
a born Goner, aunt of the missing college graduate, and
that she had married for her first husband a certain
—— Fuller. And here came another puzzle. Children by the first husband had also gone West and
were in communication with their Goner kindred, but
not one of the descendants knew the first name of
their grandmother's husband. The Fullers were a
noted family, straight from Plymouth Rock, and
they were very anxious to establish connection. I did
the best I could for them, but could find no record of
Susanna's first marriage. There were a number of
Fuller boys baptized just about the date needed, but
which was the happy man it was impossible to tell.
But chance at length leading me to consult an earlier
probate record, there I found the settlement of the
estate of Susanna's father, and among the receipts
recorded was one signed by Susanna and her Fuller
husband—*first name* and all complete. It was very
curious. She might have selected for aught we know
—Joseph, James, Samuel, Abel, John, Peter—but
with remarkable prescience the chosen name that for
so many years baffled inquiry was simply—Job—and
more than Job's patience had been expended in tracing it.]

The importance of *immediately* following up the
faintest probability cannot be too strongly urged.
If you lose your one chance what hope is left for you?
" We have these treasures in earthern vessels." Lives
and memories hang on brittle threads. Especially if
you hear of an elderly person likely to impart de-

sirable intelligence, go for him at once. So many unforeseen casualties may occur. I remember once hastening as soon as I thought decency would permit, to extract some needful item from a bereaved widower who, it was feared, would not long survive the loss of his life's companion, and the poor old soul had already skipped off with a frisky young wife upon a wedding journey. A few days delay would have left my Jay problem unsolved. Nothing surprised me more than to find a problem in this numerous and somewhat common-place family. The Jays were as plenty in town as robins and blackbirds, filling a whole district and burying-ground. A Nathaniel Jay bought up a large tract of land in that section and joined the church in due form at an early date, and I supposed in a single tramp through district and burying-ground I could pick up all family details that were needed. But behold, on the contrary, not a chatterer among them could give the least account of his ancestry, or had any knowledge or tradition of the first immigrant, Nathaniel. To be sure they could all prattle most volubly about Grandfather Jay, the popular landlord of the famous "Half-way Tavern," but he might have been Melchisedek himself for ought they knew of his origin, and so the matter rested, to my great annoyance, till Mrs. Blue Jay came chirping up to me one Sunday intermission (we did not go to the same church and met by the merest accident).

"It's not *Sunday talk*," she whispered mysteriously,
"but you know what you asked my husband, and he
has found out that Cousin Jotham out by 'The
Brass Ball' knows more about it than all the rest of
us, and after haying he is going to see him and write
it off for you."

"He need not trouble himself," I replied with my
usual briskness, "I'll see him myself to-morrow."

That a horse could have been beguiled out of the
hay-fields on such an errand was extremely doubtful,
but by rare good luck a friend needed conveyance to
an out-of-the-way station in that vicinity. It was
the loveliest of midsummer days. Passing over the
old witch-ground, so famous in local tradition, what
marvel that we were beset and hindered on our way.
The wailing spectres, phantom reapers, and headless
ghosts of other days had indeed forever vanished;
no magic deer wiled us into elusive chase over the
hill-sides—but wild roses in the freshness of "young
bud and bloom" essayed their utmost witchery; clus-
ters of rare, golden lilies beckoned into woodland
hollows; seductive strawberries gleamed out from
uncut mowing, and over-bearing raspberry bushes
fairly flung their luscious fruit into our mouths and
baskets. Bob-o-links challenged a race over the fra-
grant meadows; thickets rang with the carols of
cheery chewinks, and birds of strange plumage and
alien notes enticed as if with the very song of the si-

rens. Heroically shutting eyes and ears against these blandishments we reached the station, unscathed, in due season, whence I pursued my way alone to the farthest extremity of Jaydom, passing many a home nest, and the great old tavern where Washington took breakfast —— "That's no such rarity," you will say. "Did not he breakfast, dine, or sup, in every old tavern of the country?" But would not you like to have seen young Nathan Hale prance up to the doorstep that cold January morning in 1776, when the taverns were so crowded that he had to ride eighteen miles before he could snatch a morsel of food; or hob-a-nob-ed with Putnam, glass to glass, in the great bar-room; or bartered greetings with those valiant champions, Knowlton and Durkee; or cheered the triumphant battalions under Generals Heath and Sullivan as they marched to New York after the evacuation of Boston; or bring back for one golden hour the vanished glories of the deserted thoroughfare?

Cousin Jotham's plain farm-house recalled me to present duties. A burly old fellow, with very red face and most abnormal nose, sat by the table at the open window munching down his supper. Propounding with new hope the stereotyped query— "Can you tell me anything about the Nathaniel Jay who bought the Saltonstall tract in 1740," "Yes, I know everything about him," he interrupted. "He

was my great-grandfather, and came to this town
when grandfather Jay, his youngest child, was just
two years old." And thence he went on to report his
various wives and children, and their several husbands, wives, children, occupations, and places of
residence, as clear, methodical, and minute, as if he
had served apprenticeship at a Genealogical Bureau.
He was his grandfather's boy, he said, and used to
potter all over the farm with him, hearing his old
stories ; and so it came to pass that he alone of all the
race had treasured up the family history. And to
think that within three days after this interview this
faithful custodian should have been gathered to his
grandfathers, cut down in his own hay-field by a sun-
stroke, and if I had waited for Mr. Blue Jay to have
finished his haying, or if Mrs. Blue Jay had not
broken the Sabbath, not one of their numerous brood
might have heard this true story of their ancestors.

Finding your prospective victim alive and accessible, a word of caution may be helpful. Over rashness and precipitancy may blast your hopes in the
moment of anticipated discovery. Old people, especially those remote from the world in country places,
are easily flustered and unstrung. To burst in upon
a feeble old woman with blunt announcement of
name and errand might drive every idea and memory
from her bewildered brain, and reduce her to tempo-
rary imbecility.

"I think I *did* have a sister Olive once," whimpered a poor old lady badgered out of her wits by an unskilled evidence-taker. Gradual approach should precede the main attack. Assume an errand if you have it not. Take along your butter pail or egg basket, and from easy chat upon crops and weather glide imperceptibly into family matters, and you will hardly fail to unlock the treasures of memory and the still more precious records, carefully hoarded in Bible and pocket-book. Whatever you hear or find, do not waste time and temper in debate and argument. However absurd may be the family theory of your informants, it is not wise to controvert it. Their facts may be "first-rate" if their "theory don't coincide." You are not a judge nor partisan pleader but a seeker after truth; and what you need above all is to have every witness state whatever facts he may have, after his own light and fashion. It is just possible that his pet theory is nearer right than your own, and there are often germs of truth in the most absurd theories. More than once I have been forced to adopt views which I thought at first utterly preposterous. If you suffer pangs of conscience at leaving an ancient relative, in what seems to you gross error, consider the probable futility of attempting to enlighten him. Jokes and opiates may be injected into the system, but what can expel an idea from the fossilized intellect? Even if under the

pressure of inexorable logic you compel your oppo-
nent to admit that a man cannot die before he is born,
or be older than his grandmother, you will hear him
within twenty-four hours reiterate the same absurd-
ities. It is well, however, to insinuate mildly that
other branches of the family hold different opinions
and theories, leading your informant to a more careful scrutiny of his own position, and bringing out
more clearly all sides of the question.

These veteran hard-shells, with one or two detached facts to stand upon, are far less exasperating
than their light-minded antipodes, void alike of facts
and theories. Old people, in genealogical estimate,
are either priceless or good-for-nought. Some have
memories like a well-ordered store-house, with most
valuable commodities carefully assorted and labeled ;
while others are best typified by the household rag-
bag or refuse-heap. Truly pitiful it often seems that
eighty or ninety years' experience should have gar-
nered up so little worth preserving or repeating—and
yet it will not do to despise rag-bags and rubbish-
heaps, for precious things sometimes slip into them
that would never find their way into an orderly re-
ceptacle. Such a time as I had with old Lady
Feather-pate. The descendant of a pioneer family,
with a grandfather almost Enoch-Arden-ized by captivity in the French and Indian War, a father who
had drummed through the Revolution in Putnam's

own regiment, and personal acquaintance with all
the noted ministry and gentry of her own generation
—I could not get a tangible item out of her. Again
and again, with the utmost care and patience, I
would lead the conversation back to some noteworthy person or incident with which she must have
been perfectly familiar, and off she would bob to
some irrelevant household matter, descanting with
greatest volubility upon her success in raising *calves*,
which seemed to have been the culmination of her
life's achievement—(It was whispered, indeed, that
her own graceless cubs did her far less credit). But
amid the scum and froth of this disjointed babble
there bubbled out, inadvertently, a diamond of the
first water ; a definite, chronological, long-buried
fact, whose recovery is pronounced by my friend,
Mr. Gradgrind, of more practical value than the sum
total of all my previous investigations—a fact which
settled the original lay-out of a contested highway,
and saved two towns from angry debate and impend-
ing litigation.

This apparent dependence upon mere chance and
luck in antiquarian researches can hardly fail to
awaken anxious solicitude. If we scarcely manage
to save so many valuable items, must we not lose
many others ? Even in matters that would seem to
demand only patient plodding there is an element of
uncertainty. A gap is found in the church records

just at the time that missing great-grandmother
might have been born or married, a pivotal date by
chance left out, precious names blotted or undeci-
pherable, blundering entries, entailing inextricable
confusion and bewilderment. It is almost needless
to advise an earnest, persistent Japheth never to *send*
for information when he can possibly *go* for it, knowing as he does the risk of entrusting such search to
an indifferent person. Undoubtedly experts may be
found, especially in old mother towns, who take professional pride in unraveling the most complicated
lineage ; but the acumen of the ordinary town clerk
is, to say the least, problematic. They are often
afflicted with that peculiar optical infirmity that re-
stricts the vision to things directly under the nose.
I have known them positively deny the existence of
records that historic instinct ferreted out in five minutes. It is observed, however, that an application of
gold-dust or bank-note is a sovereign specific in such
cases. Equally uncertain is the result of epistolary
effort, the blanks, as in other lotteries, bearing a large
proportion to the prizes. Of course, all that can be
done is to try our chances over and over, believing
that an earnest seeker will in time attain the object
of search. For myself, I came at last to a certain
assured conviction that all that I needed would somehow find its way to me.

> " Nor time, nor space, nor deep, nor high,
> Can keep away my own from me !"

Ever following, never fainting, watching, hunting,
plodding, year after year, you will in time solve your
problems, fit in your links, establish connection, and
complete in a good degree your family record. Some
perverse great-grandmother or minor collateral may
yet evade you, permitting you the tantalizing pleasure of further research. Can anyone give tidings of
a certain fair Rachel, married in 1738 to a faithful
Benjamin C? Blank spaces in many "Ancestral Tablets" are waiting for her name.

[Several statements in the above paragraph need
modification and retraction. I am most happy to
affirm that the efficiency of the ordinary town official
is not in these days "problematic." On the contrary,
since the great demand for family records, the in-
efficient and blundering town clerk has become ex-
ceptional, and many of them have attained almost
preternatural acuteness in answering these demands.
The stupidity of a former fossil, who withheld for
half a dozen years the needful record from a most
importunate old gentleman simply because of one
superfluous letter in the name, cannot be paralleled
in these days. Driven to desperation, this persevering
Japheth instituted search in every town of the county, though all the evidence pointed to one particular
town. Having occasion to visit this town, I remembered his plaintive appeal, and taking up the birth-
record, there, on the very first page, inscribed in
large, bold letters with the blackest of ink, were the
names of this identical "John and Hannah," at the

precise dates specified in search warrant—with just
an o added to the family name, making it Broad instead of Brad! Anyone familiar with old records
knows that a few vowels, more or less, make no difference. There was no standard of spelling, and, first
names and date corresponding, there need have been
no doubt in this and similar cases. Most fortunately
our long suffering and waiting friend survived to
attain this welcome verification.]

The omission or displacement of some small letter
may be equally disastrous in consequences. With
deep contrition I recall the perplexity and labor inflicted upon two painstaking genealogists by inadvertently overlooking in proof the substitution of
John for Jonah and Joseph for Josiah. Both had
the sense to appeal from the printed page to previous
notes, which fortunately enabled me to correct the
error. Where old town records have been copied
there is room for many errors to creep in, unless the
copyist is familiar with old family names. In case of
doubt it is wise to consult the original record. In an
instance where the birth-date of the oldest child was
omitted from the copy, I found it safely tucked away
in the dogs-ear roll of the discarded leaf. Old ministers in baptizing a batch of babies sometimes managed to mix up the names in recording them—a source
of perplexity somewhat difficult to unravel till we
find him marrying the exchanged Lucys or Abigails
—and are able to fit them into their rightful families.

Still by care and patience we learn to, discriminate and circumvent these several errors.

And even assured success may have its reservations. It must be admitted that our ancestors are not always what we desired and expected. Some of us have to take up with Ham instead of Shem or Japheth. I have myself restored grandparents to anxious descendants when I would fain have whispered Pope's couplet:

> "Go and pretend your family is young,
>   Nor own your fathers have been fools so long."

It was embarrassing to report to an unknown applicant from *Boston*, that one of the name had been publicly flogged at the whipping post for breaking the Sabbath; that another had figured as a witch, sticking pins into sleeping neighbors, and committing other malicious pranks; and a third, bearing the same unlucky name, was the last man *hung* in the county! One letter of inquiry among hundreds that have come to me is left unanswered, my pen refusing to blast the hopes of the wife of a high church dignitary by the disgraceful intelligence that the last heard of her unworthy progenitor he had been convicted of horse-stealing, whipped, branded, and sent back to jail for lack of means to pay the fine. Let him rest in dark oblivion. An ancestor with no more consideration for the feelings of descendants deserves to be blotted from their record.

[I feel now that I was utterly at fault in the above premises and conclusion. Under present light and experience I feel that the inquirer should be informed of every fact connected with his family history, and that the genealogist has no right to keep back discoveries, however unfavorable.]

" From Nature's chain whatever link you strike,
    Tenth or ten-thousandth breaks the chain alike."

If one link was unsound, those back of it may have proved of true metal. How great the loss inflicted in this particular instance can never be determined. My horse-lifter may have come from some robber count or highland freebooter; he may have descended, like myself, from William the Conqueror or a line of raiding Vikings, and by withholding this link I have robbed the Bishop's children of ability to prove connection.   We wish, like good Mr. Omer, " that parties were brought up stronger minded," so that the genealogist need not feel qualmish in making disagreeable revelations.   It is certainly absurd for citizens of our great republic to be unduly squeamish concerning the social position of their ancestors.   We cannot " all be corporals " as the children expected in the old story, and may take rightful pride in having worked our way up from the ranks by dint of honest struggle and gradual promotion. Even the honor and privilege of tracing your line straight back to historic names brought over in the Mayflower, or Winthrop's fleet, has its drawbacks.

"What a *descent*," said a sarcastic old gentleman
to a boastful scion of the Pilgrims. A less noted
line may also portend a more vigorous future. Families, like their familiar symbol, grow, culminate, and
decay. Your old trees have hollow trunks and many
sapless, moss-grown branches. Some are blighted,
some quickened by change of position and climate.

" A tree that stands square in old Massachusetts,
   When transplanted to other States sometimes askew sets."

The most hopelessly inert, lifeless, incapable specimens of humanity may be found among the descendants of old Puritan magnates. And while there are
those who still do honor to illustrious names, it must
be admitted that it is the new blood that chiefly leads
in public affairs. Over fruitfulness in past genera-
tions may have impaired capacity for present pro-
duction, and the lower the social position of your
grandfather the better may be the chance for your
grandson's future.

But there are things unearthed by the genealogist
harder to bear than degree of social position. There
are " blots on the escutcheon," bar-sinisters, too great
discrepancy between dates of birth and marriage, in
some instances birth preceding marriage. Those
familiar with ancient church records find frequent
examples of such previousness. The custom of ex-
torting a public confession from such offenders would

seem to have aggravated the evil, making it almost
a matter of course that such confession should be
needed. With our ideas of the strictness of Puritan
morals and discipline, it seems remarkable that such
a condition of things should have existed; yet in
point of fact, it was less immoral than appears on the
surface, and was based on the old Germanic idea of
the sacredness of the betrothal. "Engaged folks
have a right to live like married ones," was the blunt
assertion of one sturdy recusant. The poverty of the
times, the lack of business openings, made it difficult
for a young man to provide and maintain an independent household, and existing customs allowed
great liberty of intercourse between contracting
parties. In one case, at least, marriage was delayed
till the youngster was old enough to be the most conspicuous witness of the ceremony. It may be said
that this liberty was seldom abused, and that instances where marriage did not follow this previous
intercourse are very infrequent. But when for some
unavoidable cause marriage was prevented, it bore
most hardly upon the unmarried mother, bearing
through life a burden of disgrace and sorrow, having
lapsed no more than hundreds of more fortunate
sisters who lived and died in honor. On the other
side, a pathetic incident occurred in the death of a
young mother soon after the birth of her child. The
infant was baptized at its dying mother's bedside,

but almost immediately the father had its birth recorded under his own name, and his family assumed
its charge and support. But a shadow followed the
young man through life. When, after a time, he decided to marry, his first child was given the name of
his lost love, and his life ends in a mazy tradition of
falling over a bridge in mist and darkness. In that
case, as in many others, marriage had been delayed
simply as a matter of convenience.

But in the days following the Revolution there was
far greater looseness of morals and manners. It was
a time of general upheaval and commotion. The
deadness of the established churches, the spread of
French Revolution ideas and infidelity, the assertion
of personal liberty, and the excessive use of liquor, all
conspired to induce a very bad condition of affairs.
The diary of our friend Zeph gives a graphic picture
of the frolickings and junketings among young people of his grade, and among his many frank entries
are those of numerous births immediately preceding,
or without, marriage. Nor were things much better
among the higher classes. That such a graceless rep-
robate as Oliver Dodge could have maintained his
position in such a town as Pomfret, shows the low
tone of public morals. Our first ventures in popular literature bear striking testimony in this line.
Ministers' sons and deacons' daughters, teachers in
Plainfield Academy and promising young lawyers,

figure in highly sensational stories, with only too
much literal foundation. With the new century
came new spiritual life and movements, and influences were set at work that wrought a wonderful
betterment in all directions. If any genealogical
Japheth lights upon an unfavorable record, or lack
of record, during this unsavory period, he can only
comfort himself by the probability that many others
are in the same situation. The genealogist may
deem himself fortunate who never stumbles upon an
unpleasant revelation. "Any possible move," says
the wise Mr. Bucket, "being a probable move according to my experience." Considering all the bad
things that have been done in the world, we have no
right to claim exemption for our ancestors. And the
farther back we go the greater probability of wrong-
doing. It is all very well to trace your line back into
the old world, intersecting lines of nobility and kings,
but their character and conduct will not bear close
inspection. A line or lines straight back without
gap or blot to substantial New England settlers is
as good a thing as one need have in the way of ancestry, and many such favored lines have been tri-
umphantly established, while failure in any point
certainly demands great exercise of philosophy.

But if you have not gained all that you would like,
your search has not been fruitless. Apart from the
fascinating excitement of pursuit it has strengthened

the ties of blood and kindred, and given you a closer apprehension of the oneness of the human family. Amid the hurry and rush of our headlong national growth and expansion this modern interest in genealogical research has a most beneficent and humanizing influence, counteracting the tendency to separation and dispersion, and drawing thousands of scattered families around a common hearthstone. Most noteworthy is its bearing upon the vexed question of New England's future. At a time when the outflow of its native population and the influx of foreigners has revolutionized the rural district, when a great majority of Yankee farms are tilled by those of alien blood and tongue, this awakened interest in ancestral homes and shrines is a hopeful feature in the situation. Pilgrim sons of Pilgrim fathers pay pious visits to the graves of their ancestors, and arrange for their better care and more fitting memorial stone or tablet. Often the interest extends to the family homestead, the neighborhood, the town, and finds expression in helpful aid—in renovated church-yard and church edifice; in public schoolhouse or library building. Many a town has received a new impulse from these friendly gifts, arousing the before discouraged residents to greater efforts in their own behalf, and stimulating the interest and coöperation of other wandering sons and old-time residents. Family reunions at ancestral homes,

bringing together sons and daughters from all parts
of the land, strengthen the ties of blood and early
association, and make it more and more evident that
sons of New England will not outgrow their filial
relations; that the homes that nourished the infancy
of our land will be even more honored and cherished
as time rolls on.

And in its more personal aspect the genealogist
finds great reward. His feeling of kinship widens
out to the whole family circle and brings them into
reciprocal relations. Truly "he setteth the solitary
in families." To many isolated lives he brings new
sources of interest and consolation. The most shriveled old maid, the dryest old twig of a bachelor,
gains new life and freshness when incorporated into
a family tree. To how many of our elderly friends
this pursuit has brought enjoyment that nothing else
could substitute. How striking its adaptation to the
instinctive craving of those, who retired from active
labor, can thus gather up the past and project it into
the future:

> " Becoming, as is meet and fit,
> A link among the days, to knit
> The generations, each to each."

How hopeful the interest and enthusiasm thus
awakened among the younger branches.

Success to all the Japheths, far and near! May
each achieve his "Tree," and may its shadow never
be less.

INDEX.

BIBLIOBAZAAR

The essential book market!

Did you know that you can get any of our titles in our trademark **EasyRead**[TM] print format? **EasyRead**[TM] provides readers with a larger than average typeface, for a reading experience that's easier on the eyes.

Did you know that we have an ever-growing collection of books in many languages?

Order online:
www.bibliobazaar.com

Or to exclusively browse our **EasyRead**[TM] collection:
www.bibliogrande.com

At BiblioBazaar, we aim to make knowledge more accessible by making thousands of titles available to you – quickly and affordably.

Contact us:
BiblioBazaar
PO Box 21206
Charleston, SC 29413

Printed in the United States
142734LV00001B/22/A